To CHARLES ⟨...⟩ ⟨...⟩GR

W⟨...⟩

Ya⟨...⟩

Bob Garratt

26 June 1996

LONDON

THE FISH
ROTS
FROM THE
HEAD

THE FISH ROTS FROM THE HEAD

•

The Crisis in Our Boardrooms:
Developing the Crucial Skills of
the Competent Director

BOB GARRATT

HarperCollinsBusiness

HarperCollinsBusiness
An imprint of HarperCollins*Publishers*
77–85 Fulham Palace Road,
Hammersmith, London W6 8JB

Published by HarperCollins*Business* 1996
1 3 5 7 9 8 6 4 2

A catalogue record for this book
is available from the British Library

ISBN 0 00 255613 8

Set in Linotype Sabon by
Rowland Phototypesetting Ltd,
Bury St Edmunds, Suffolk

Printed and bound in Great Britain by
Caledonian International Book Manufacturing Ltd, Glasgow

In memory of Christopher Lorenz

Contents

Figures

Tables

A Note on Style and Sources

Most organizations around the world use the term 'director' to describe members of their governing board, but I am aware that, particularly in the United States, the term 'president' or 'vice president' is used instead, and the term 'director' refers to a level of management directly below that. For years I have asked why 'president'. No-one really seems to know, but the most common answer I have had is that it relates back to the nineteenth-century 'robber barons' who effectively established themselves above, or beyond, government and legislative controls. However, I have used the term 'director' when referring to all corporate governance systems including the US.

I have used the term 'independent director' wherever possible to replace the more negative-sounding 'non-executive director'. I have done this more in hope than as a reflection of current reality. I realize that at present many 'independent' directors are not truly independent. It is a key challenge for corporate governance in the twenty-first century to ensure that they become so.

I have used the term 'chairman' throughout to denote the person who is boss of the board – the person who chairs the board processes. A large number of my clients are women and all of them use this term proudly. They object strongly to being addressed as 'chair' because they are not an inanimate object for sitting on; far from it. I stand by their judgement. It is a term which causes much more fuss outside the boardroom than in it.

I have used numerous examples throughout the book, mainly from my own experience. In most cases I have simplified them to stress the main point. These 'sanitized' versions do not reflect the full complexity of the issues involved.

This book is not designed as an instruction manual. Given the breadth of its coverage it cannot be. I have attempted to bring together the best ideas and practice I have seen around the world.

Whilst I can claim some ownership and responsibility for the Learning Board concept, most of the other information in this book comes from my own 'environmental scanning' of easily available sources, mostly newspapers. I hope that it proves the point that such environmental scanning is productive. Furthermore it is enjoyable, consumes little time, is easy to learn – and means that you and your board will be sensitive enough to 'hear the baby cry'. If you want to know what that means, read on.

Introduction

Have you ever questioned the fact that so many organization charts start with the chief executive and work downwards? Or that we keep the interplay of ownership and executive power in our organizations secret? Are you happy with what happens around the boardroom table? It is currently less than most of us would expect. Do you know what *should* be happening around the boardroom table? Are you aware of the potentially huge positive effects truly competent boards could have on our private companies and public services?

Some enterprises are beginning to tackle these issues. The majority are not. This book sets out to illuminate the ideas and processes by which it is possible for a board to get to grips with issues that are becoming increasingly crucial to organizational success. It is devoted to those boards of directors who are not 'competent'. This is not to say that they are *incompetent*, but rather that they have not been through the training, induction or inclusion processes necessary in order to make the transition from managers to direction-givers.

This is an international problem. Across the world newspapers have been full of dramatic corporate governance stories, glaring examples of alleged incompetence and corruption, showing that all is not well at the top of our enterprises, public or private. In the UK, directors have been accused of failing in their duties, as in the recent Maxwell case and the Barings crisis. In Italy and France, world-renowned figures have been arrested for illegal payments to political parties. In Germany, there have been allegations of corruption at Schneider and Adam Opel. In the USA the allegations have been of incompetence at the highest levels in corporations that were world-beaters in the 1960s and 70s, such as IBM and General Motors, and in Japan, the scandals reported have included corrupt business links with political parties, or the trading losses at Daiwa.

These and the stories of massive pay-rises, the awarding of stock options and other benefits despite unimpressive company performance, and of large payments to executives through service contracts following dismissal for underperformance have opened up a furious global debate about the nature of corporate governance and the accountability of the board. There is little confidence that the interests of shareholders, large or small, or stakeholders, whether they be staff, customers, suppliers, local communities or the physical environment, are being looked after satisfactorily.

Governments are struggling to come to terms with the growing public disquiet. In the UK the Cadbury and Greenbury Committees have focused debate. France has the Viénot Report. German corporate governance was spotlighted in a 1995 OECD report, the Hong Kong Stock Exchange has published 'Guidelines for Directors', Australia is worrying over the result of the AWA case and both the United States and Japan are beginning to take their situations seriously as a result of growing criticism from institutional shareholders.

I believe that the shortcomings in organizations arise because of the overemphasis on managing, or being a professional, and the consequent underemphasis on *directing* – showing the way ahead and giving leadership. A corporation needs effective management to keep its day-to-day operations running, but to ensure that it sustains itself in its long-term energy niches – the complex web of customers, suppliers, staff, local communities, and the changing political, physical, economic, social, technological and trade environments that feed its business – it needs effective directing too. If this is not recognized by the board of directors, incompetence and corruption can multiply. As the Chinese saying goes, 'The fish rots from the head.' Whether or not this is physiologically correct, it is a powerful metaphor for the board to consider.

How many of your board, executive or independent directors, have had any training or development for their *direction-giving* role, rather than their management role, other than vaguely defined 'experience'? If this is more than ten percent, then you are on the side of the angels. In a survey conducted by the Institute of Directors in 1990, ninety-two percent of board directors – a figure reflected in all the major trading nations of the world – said they had had no training or induction into their directoral role. It is no surprise that most boards cannot spell out their main roles or tasks.

As I see it, the key to organizational health is a thoughtful and committed board of directors, *not* managers, at the heart of the enterprise. It is the board's job to keep striking balances between the external and internal pressures on the organization to ensure its survival. The board must give a clear direction to the business and create the emotional climate in which its people can align and attune to that direction. It is the board's job to ensure that sufficient numbers of members are pointing in the same direction, committed to a common purpose, with similar values and behaviours, so that the organization can function effectively and efficiently.

Worryingly, under present institutional and legal structures, it is only in a crisis that directors might, much too late, become aware of what is required of them. Besides the fact that the health and future of any organization depends on good direction from the board, it is essential to grasp that each member of a board is not only corporately but also *personally* responsible and liable financially for the duties and tasks of the board. So far litigation has been quite light in this area, but it is rapidly getting tougher as the public perception of directors worsens. As personal liability claims become more frequent and grow in size, so the need to be sufficiently competent as a director increases, if you are to protect your personal wealth. The insurance companies cannot cover everything. Understanding one's contribution to the board is crucial.

In many ways it is hardly surprising that directors do not expand into their role, since being awarded a directorship is too often seen only as the prize at the end of a successful managerial or professional career. The new director is given a significant rise in salary and benefits, the Jaguar, BMW, Cadillac or Lexus, the service contract, stock options and congratulations by a grateful company and family. They feel wonderful and do not ask too many questions about the corporate and personal responsibilities and liabilities into which they have entered, the roles and tasks that are demanded of them, or even how they can make their best personal contribution to the board. Nor are they encouraged to.

But there is a vast difference between 'directing' and 'managing' an organization. Managing is literally, given its Latin root, a hands-on activity thriving on crises and action. On the operations side of an organization it is a crucial role. Directing is different. Directing is essentially an intellectual activity. It is about showing the way ahead, giving leadership. It is thoughtful and reflective and requires the acquisition by each director of a portfolio of completely different *thinking* skills.

Both managing and directing are necessary for a healthy enterprise. As we have invested so much of our working lives in managing, or exercising our professional skills, we are often loath to have to put more energy into doing something quite new – giving direction. But the need for direction-giving does not diminish with the size of the business, the turnover of the company, whether it is profit making or non-profit making, whether it is in the private or public sector, or whether it is a family business or professional practice.

The end of the twentieth century has seen a traumatic period in the roles of private and public organizations as key stabilizing institutions in our society. We have seen massive drops in the employment of full-time employees. During the late 1970s the majority of the people made redundant were blue-collar workers. From the late 1980s structural economic and macro-political changes – the end of the Cold War, the start of the Age of Uncertainty in the West – plus huge advances in the capabilities of computing power have given rise to the implosion of management in organizations. Between 1988 and 1993 around half of the people made redundant in the European Union were managers. Suitable euphemisms were found by top managers to explain this radical force – 'downsizing', 're-engineering', 'rightsizing', 'delayering' amongst many.

The idea was that slim, lean, responsive, customer-friendly organizations should be created in the private and public sectors. With a few notable exceptions this has not happened; the reverse is usually true. What it was hoped would be a high-level integration process has usually become a low-level organizational compromise. Organizations which have been 'slimmed' ruthlessly now tend to house undertrained, inexperienced, risk-averse workers and managers fearsome of losing their jobs. Unthinking redundancy programmes often lose the crucial experience base of the organization so that it can no longer respond to sudden changes in its environment. Customers' perceptions of 'good value for money' for the product or service are damaged and can give rise to customer cynicism of the 'more means less' variety. It is very easy for thoughtless senior managers to reduce a healthy organization to an anorexic, or bulimic, one. The former is obsessed with slimming and 'bottom lines' to the point where any problem is dealt with by slimming again, until the inevitable organizational death. The latter binges on managerial fashions, then throws up and starts again. Neither ensures long-term corporate health. It is the directors' task to create the long-term vision which puts such fads in perspective.

Most newly appointed directors realize that they do need to acquire new attitudes, knowledge and skills to handle these higher-level issues. However, they are often frightened to ask for help as they feel that by doing so they will expose their non-competence and so risk demotion or sacking. Other newly-appointed directors are actively hostile to the idea that they should learn how to do a 'new' job. They feel they are too old to start again, and that they have done their bit for the company as a manager. They have now earned their comfortable place on the board.

For all these reasons most directors do not recognize, or do not accept, what the director's job demands from them. This is where the directoral learning blockage starts. It is to these directors that this book is addressed.

CHAPTER 1

Directing, Not Managing

Managers have acted effectively as the agents of owners ever since the size of organizations became impossible for individuals or families to control. Heavily influenced by the industrial production model created by Henry Ford, managers saw their role as breaking organizations into functional chunks which were then broken down to the minimum size for each piece of work. These 'manageable' activities would then be set their output targets within work-group plans, which would be scaled up to create a corporate masterplan.

Such bureaucratic thinking and design have been effective for most of the twentieth century, while the external environment has been reasonably stable. But now that predictability is breaking down. Great confusion is found in boards both about the external macro-politics and at the internal organizational level in an attempt to cope with these changes.

Much of the current executive thinking is framed around 'decentralizing' or demolishing headquarters' functions, 'flattening' organizations to just four to six distinct organizational levels, 'downsizing', 'outsourcing', or imploding the managerial functions and 'empowering' the shell-shocked work force to drive out cost and make the organization more effective. These 'strategies' are usually not thought through or are implemented in patently contradictory ways. If these are responses to an increasingly more chaotic and turbulent world, what is the intellectual basis of them? Will they help their organizations to survive and develop into the twenty-first century? I doubt it, because the dynamic balance between organizational efficiency and organizational effectiveness is not understood.

The important, but oversimplistic, notion that the only certainty now is change is not particularly helpful here. The tendency to flatten, or work towards 'federations' and 'corporate democracies' like ABB (Asea Brown Boveri), who have achieved this successfully, seems in the huge majority of cases to happen without any integrated long-term political, environmental, economic, social, technological, and trade thoughts to orientate the organization, nor any explicit corporate purpose, 'Vision and Values' or ethics to guide it.

DIRECTING AS A PROPER JOB

It is essential that the board learns how to cope with the difficult, messy uncertainty of these issues in rigorous and self-disciplined ways. A board of directors must budget time to incorporate in a measured way all the aspects it should be dealing with in its working year. Only then will the rest of the organization gain from its leadership, and so be able to learn to self-manage, to reach the targets, budgets, and milestones which create the shareholder value for the next period of performance. The problem is that virtually all the boards I have seen do not so time-budget, because they do not see directing as a 'proper' job. It is often seen as an add-on luxury to be fitted in after the real work of managing is done.

Many 'manager/directors' feel much more comfortable with just managing, or exercising their professional discipline. After all, it was good performance as a manager or professional that earned them the position of director. Some of the younger, rapidly promoted ones may feel a bit puzzled as to how they will spend the rest of their working lives, but most feel that they are there, not, primarily, to give direction, but to ensure that their managerial successor does not mess up what they have so painfully achieved.

They have an understandable, but not forgivable, inclination to find any excuse to intervene in the managerial system as soon as they see a crisis occurring, or to create a crisis themselves so that they can continue to demonstrate their managerial prowess.

Direction-givers need a 'brain-on', rather than a 'hands-on' attitude. Theirs should be a thoughtful world from which they delegate authority to managers to design and deliver the operational parts of the enterprise. Directors need to create the political, strategic and emotional environment for this to happen but they must give their highest priority to ensuring that their organization is supported in its energy niches, or can migrate to new ones so that it can continue to survive and grow.

A change of directoral mindset is needed. Directors usually see themselves as sitting at the apex of a pyramid and do not look beyond themselves to the outside world. They need instead to see themselves as the centre of the enterprise – the 'business brain' or central processor – monitoring and coping with the results of the external *and* internal learning processes of the whole enterprise.

Four Dynamic Balances

The basic ecological system in which a board must find and maintain its energy niches can be defined by four opposing forces which have to be balanced against each other. A key task of the board of directors under the ultimate responsibility of the chairman is to create sufficient space to maintain a continuous overview of these:

1. Organizational Effectiveness
The external, long-term perception in the customer's mind of the products or services being desirable and good value for money.

2. Organizational Efficiency

The internal, short-term focus on cost reduction and efficiency gain – but only until just before it affects negatively the customer's perception of organizational effectiveness.

3. Board Performance

The external focus of the board on policy formulation in relation to the external 'political' environments; and on strategic thinking about the competitive positioning and broad resource allocation of the enterprise in relation to its policies.

4. Board Conformance

The internal focus of the board on its performance to pre-set goals of accountability to its stakeholders; and to its business performance through its people.

Each of these four forces has the potential to be in contradiction to each of the others.

In order for boards to achieve the changes in their mindset, there should be a conscious board development process, under the eye of the chairman, starting with induction, inclusion, and training to competence. According to the surveys undertaken, the Institute of Director's *Development of and for the Board* [1] and my own experience, this rarely happens. What tends to occur is that, on promotion to the role of director, the new appointee is told 'Well done! Now just turn up and shut up. Come to the board meetings, of course. But don't ask too many questions. Don't rock the boat. You'll pick it up as you go along.' There is little induction: no paperwork to outline the job (even when the local stock exchange says that there should be), nor to outline the corporate and personal responsibilities and liabilities, and no offer of help to make the transition effectively from managing or being a professional to directing.

If there is little induction, there is even less inclusion. The 'turn up and shut up' message is strong even from a board in crisis, and it takes a very strong-minded individual to have enough self-confidence and independence of mind to keep asking discriminating questions until he or she gets satisfactory answers. If it is difficult enough for an independent director, it often seems impossible for a recently promoted executive director. Yet asking discriminating questions is a key directoral skill, and the wish to ask them a necessary attitude. Asking 'intelligently naive' questions is what the directoral job is about, whether of the internal management and operational systems or of the external environment. The ability to use intelligence in asking fundamental questions, and not to be put off by the functional specialists' 'technobabble', is what directors are paid to do.

This can come as a shock to existing directors who are settled deep into the cosy 'club culture' of a board and have no wish to be excluded. Such behaviour is a sure sign that they are underperforming in their directoral roles. They are not creating sufficient diversity in their questioning and thinking to keep up with the rate of change in their external environment. Their enterprise will not be able to stay within its energy-sustaining niches.

Inclusion, which at its best means recognizing the added diversity the newcomer brings to the capacity of the board as the corporate brain, is a fundamental human need. The process by which this happens can be quite bizarre and is unique to each board. I know of one major international company where the chairman is also a British gentleman farmer. His major means of controlling his board – the independent directors are a powerful group of individuals in their own right – is the award of one of his homemade cheeses each December. He does not necessarily give one to each board member every year, so the board directors tend to be acquiescent during October and November as each tries to ensure that they are included by the chairman. Logically this is nonsense. The independent directors all have major jobs elsewhere, and the executive directors have powerful egos. Emotionally, however, it is understandable. Boards are composed of human beings who need recognition.

It may be understandable that people wish to work with others like themselves, but the danger is that this can easily lead to 'cloning' – and insufficient diversity of thought – as exemplified in the table below.

Table 1 Is your board a club? A survey of UK boards

	Retail	Finance	Engineering	Food and Drink
Dimension of Diversity %				
Board members over 50	64	80	76	80
Women board members	8	4	3	0
Non-UK members	7	5	10	18
Attended public school	42	37	53	40
Attended Oxbridge	16	26	17	20
Board members with public sector experience	15	16	26	10
Career primarily in one organization	28	16	26	57
Board member for more than 5 years	52	33	36	44
Board members with international experience	17	24	25	38
Board members holding other directorships	47	55	75	68

Source: Sundridge Park Corporate Research, UK, 1994

THE BOARD'S ROLES

The publication in 1995 of *Standards for the Board* by the Institute of Directors (IOD), London, via a government-sponsored survey was extraordinary for two main reasons. First, that it took the IOD, founded in 1903 and granted a Royal Charter in 1906, until 1995 to state what a board actually does. *Standards for the Board* is a great step forward. Before its publication, boards were often meant to absorb osmotically their roles and tasks and usually did it badly. Second, *Standards* defines new thinking and good practice for boards and is a positive response to the bad press about corporate governance issues. It is proving to be a driving force in setting in motion a worldwide debate on the roles and tasks of a board, and on the need to link training and assessed competence with membership of directors' professional bodies.

The Four Directoral Dilemmas

Standards for the Board lays out clearly what I call the four 'Directoral Dilemmas':

1. The board must simultaneously be entrepreneurial and drive the business forward whilst keeping it under prudent control.
2. The board is required to be sufficiently knowledgeable about the workings of the company to be answerable for its actions, and yet to stand back from the day-to-day management and retain an objective, longer-term view.
3. The board must be sensitive to the pressures of short-term, local issues and yet be informed of the broader trends and competition, often of an international nature.
4. The board is expected to be focused on the commercial needs of the business whilst acting responsibly towards its employees, business partners, and society as a whole.

These are massive expectations of any board and demand a diversity, in terms of breadth and depth of experience, knowledge, attitudes and skills, which cannot be expected of any one individual, no matter how powerful. That is why we have a *board* of directors. In theory a board is a collegiate activity – all members are equal. A board should not be the province of any one powerful individual, because over time they inevitably pass their 'use-by' date and then become a negative influence on the enterprise.

To make matters more complex, each role mentioned above seems to be a contradiction in itself. Let's look at each in turn.

First, that the board be entrepreneurial and yet keep prudent control demands both a 'performing' and a 'conforming' board. 'Entrepreneurial' does not have a strictly commercial meaning, but for most organizations it is the commercial aspects which exercise them. So a board has to be adventurous and risk-taking to keep up with the energy-niche changes in its external environment, and yet has a legal 'fiduciary duty' to hold the company in trust on behalf of the owners.

Second, having sufficient knowledge of the workings of the company to be answerable for its actions to the owners and auditors, and yet having the intellectual capacity to stand back and take a long-term, objective view of the business, is intimidating to many directors. This area alone can put great stress on the newly-appointed director who has come up a specialist managerial or professional route, because the bureaucratic division of organizations has often led to a sealing off of one managerial function from another. New executive directors from within the business can have great difficulty understanding the roles and jargon of the other functions, yet are reluctant to question them at the board, because they do not want to seem ignorant, and because they want to encourage others not to question them too deeply in return. In doing so they miss the opportunity to rise above the single-function perspective and develop the crucial 'helicopter view' ability necessary for direction-givers.

Third, we are all tempted to get overinvolved with short-term, local issues whilst avoiding the intellectual stretch of having to set a context that takes broad trends and international competition into serious consideration. The short term can feel like 'real' work rather more than abstract speculation. However, the abstraction is crucial to effective direction-giving.

Finally, having to ensure that the commercial needs of the business are secure whilst acting responsibly towards employees, business partners, customers, suppliers and society in general can really turn off some directors, especially those who feel their only task is to generate profit for the shareholders.

These four Directoral Dilemmas are the core concerns of this book. It is possible – and essential – to move a board from the usual management-crisis fixation through rigorous board and personal training and development processes to becoming a Learning Board – a board capable of positioning itself between the external and internal cycles of learning, and integrating both. Few boards have achieved this yet. But boards around the world are now acknowledging the need to learn how to.

Sadly, many board members raise their eyes and hands in horror at the idea of coping with the four Dilemmas and then, keeping the benefits package and status of a director, unofficially drop back into their old job in the managerial, or professional, world. This feels very comfortable, particularly if there is a crisis around to sort out. You are back doing real work which you know well and which got you promoted. But this common, and understandable, behaviour by directors leads to two types of debilitating organizational problem.

First, the person who has your old job, or its equivalent, usually will not take lightly your sitting on their shoulders saying what has to be done. This leads to a lot of heat and not much light being shed on matters, since the present job-holder has their own views and experience which are as valid as yours – and it is they, after all, who have the functional responsibility for that job. Eventually either the junior leaves or, more often, he or she moves down a level themselves and starts doing the job of the person below them, causing a similar set of problems. This has a knock-on effect down the organization until a culture of blocked development and non-competence is created. The organization is well on the way to becoming a non-learning organization. This is a common phenomenon all over the world and can be measured through the use of, for example, an 'organizational climate survey', in which people often report that they are paid one or two levels above the job they actually do. This is bad for both organizational effectiveness and efficiency.

Second, abdication of the directoral role in favour of the managerial or professional role leaves one or two powerful individuals to run the board and the business. In the USA this is still considered a good thing, and most chief executives demand it, but in many other parts of the world they have learned the hard way that this can be highly dangerous to the long-term health of the organization. Such concentration of power in the hands of a few leads eventually to absolute corruption, whether we are talking about a US transitional, a UK family company, an East Asian multinational or a Communist state enterprise. The public perception that a company is being run by one powerful individual is often alarmingly correct. But can a person be such a paragon of excellence that they are capable of undertaking all board tasks and roles simultaneously?

No. Over a period of around seven years, absolute power will corrupt, and without a diverse, questioning board the organization will collapse because of the individual's own internal contradictions.

It is worth remembering John Argenti's *Symptoms of Corporate Collapse*[2] as a caveat for all boards of directors. In my twenty-one years in director development around the world, everyone has recognized the truth in this list. It illustrates the perennial problems of board selection, working and development.

Symptoms of Corporate Collapse

One-man rule
A non-participating board
An unbalanced top team
A lack of management depth
A weak finance function
A combined chairman and chief executive role.

If we look at this list in detail some important points emerge.

1. ONE-MAN RULE

An individual man or woman who achieves absolute corporate power can be highly beneficial in the short term – in the start-up, rapid development, or crisis resolution modes for example. But as the organization stabilizes, such power will inevitably become organizationally disabling if it is not challenged, constructively criticized and debated continuously. That is the board's role. Psychometric tests show that it makes little difference whether the individual is a man or a woman. My latest inventories from East Asia show that very powerful women, owner-directors or executive agents of the shareholders, have similar profiles to men at this level.

2. A NON-PARTICIPATING BOARD

This is the antithesis of a Learning Board. Most non-participating boards that I have seen tend to stick closely to a legally-orientated and constrained framework where company secretarial issues are given as much priority as any information or debate on board performance or organizational effectiveness. The full implications of 'participation' on a board take some working through and learning about by its members. Participation has two roots from its Latin base – joint ownership, and joint responsibility. Deciding who 'owns' what on the board – power, roles and tasks – is a key part of organizing the board. Deciding the nature of joint responsibility is, at least in one way, much easier: all directors are ultimately equally responsible.

In most legislations around the world there is no legal differentiation between an independent and an executive director. This does not always go down well with a board that is made up of a group of powerful individuals, all of whom are used to getting their own way, and all of whom are skilled at covering up problems and mistakes. To insist that at board level they are legally equal is a difficult but necessary task for the chairman. The executive directors are, until properly inducted and included, unlikely to argue or debate with their boss – the chief executive. Neither are they likely to be happy constructively questioning and criticizing each other, as 'no poaching' agreements will usually be in force, explicitly or implicitly. Independent directors are often more open to debate and participation, but can easily be excluded by the 'technobabble' of the executive directors. The role of the chairman as the 'boss of the board' is crucial here to ensure an open debate and the reasonable exercise of power.

3. AN 'UNBALANCED' TOP TEAM

'Unbalanced' does not mean that the board is barking mad, although I have my doubts over some. It refers to the tendency to 'clone'. In other words, too many of the same types of people – similar in age, sex, educational background, professional training, social background and so on – come together on the board. This is written large in some corporations, some family businesses, and many professional practices. It discourages participation, particularly when questioning the working assumptions and the sources and validity of information about the changing internal and external environments on which the board is working. In such cases there is not sufficient diversity amongst its members to ensure a broad view.

4. A LACK OF MANAGEMENT DEPTH

This is also alluded to in the IOD *Standards*. The board must know enough about what is going on inside the organization and with customers to be 'answerable for its actions'. It must also demonstrate its 'fiduciary duties' in such a way that it ensures that the assets of the business are held properly in trust for the owners. Again, the capacity of the board to pose discriminating questions to the operations people until they understand and are satisfied with their answers is a crucial board discipline.

5. A WEAK FINANCE FUNCTION

This is still a problem in most companies despite all the improvements in accounting practice and information systems over the years. Many directors have never learned that businesses fail ultimately when they run out of cash. This happens depressingly frequently. Even when 'cash is king' many directors do not understand the relationships between volume, cost, and price when the business is running. Although such concerns are operational and, therefore, part of the managerial world, they often have strategic implications and so need to be understood by the directors. As better quality management information systems are appearing, it is less likely that the finance function will be as weak as before, but thoughtless, non-learning businesses will still run out of cash.

6. A COMBINED CHAIRMAN AND CHIEF
EXECUTIVE ROLE

The killer blow for an enterprise is often one person holding the very different jobs of chairman and chief executive, especially if this is for a sustained time, because there is no forum for criticism, constructive or otherwise. The chairman's job is to design and chair the process of the board's meetings and subsequent activities. The chief executive's role is to run the business. They are both powerful positions and the two people concerned need, therefore, a mutual respect and to agree a way of working together. If this is not the case then the power balance swings unhealthily and the directors are left with a lop-sided board: either the chairman tries to run the total business, or the chief executive tries to run the business, deal with the crises, and still find plenty of time to think reflectively about the long term. Neither situation is satisfactory because neither person can do both.

In the ideal world the board is trying to steer between the Scylla of the executive director-dominated board with its overemphasis on operational matters, and the Charybdis of the independent director-dominated board with its overemphasis on policy formulation at the expense of operational concerns.

The Peter Principle[3] of people being promoted to their level of incompetence is only true if there is no process for inducting, including and training to competence existing and potential board members. A leading US company president said of his board in a throwaway line that they were his 'pet rocks'. In my talks and work in the USA I have been unpleasantly surprised at the number of times I have been told that a US board of directors comprises 'ten friends of the chief executive, a woman, and a black'.

The traditional 'joke' stereotype of the board is, 'The unworthy appointed by the unwilling for the unnecessary.' 'Just remember, Bob,' a cynical trades union official reminded me when discussing board selection, 'both the cream and the scum rise to the top.' This must be fought against.

The aim must be to develop both a board and an organization capable of learning continuously from what is occurring internally and externally around them. Only by so doing can the board reflect upon, and take action on, the pressures inside and outside the organization and so encourage the organization to continuously renew itself.

CHAPTER • 2

The Learning Board

CAN YOUR ORGANIZATION LEARN?

For organizations to survive and grow, their rate of learning has to be equal to, or greater than, the rate of change in their environment. Revan's axiom – $L \geq C$ – is an essential of organizational ecology. It is easy to state, easy to agree with, but difficult to implement. Yet it must be implemented if the enterprise is to continue to exist and develop. Good examples of organizations recognizing the importance of continuous learning are Intel and Microsoft in computing, Marks & Spencer and Wal-Mart in retailing, and British Airways and Harley Davidson in travel.

All members of an organization need to understand that to achieve this happy state there must be systems for comparing regularly what is happening outside the organization, by monitoring the external environment, benchmarking and competitor analysis, and what is happening internally, through comparing customer satisfaction, productivity and financial ratios with policies, strategies, plans, budgets and projects. Comparison, reflection and action help to build people's experience and show them the benefits of continuing to learn.

Moments of Truth

The key to encouraging such learning is in getting the people of the organization to behave as though they were not part of the traditional organizational pyramid, with the owners and the directors at the top and the unskilled workers at the bottom. This is not how the customer experiences the organization from outside, and it is the customer who decides whether to buy the product or service and, more importantly, whether to make a repeat buy – which determines ultimately whether you have a job or not.

Customers have 'moments of truth'[4] with your enterprise when they telephone in, when the maintenance person arrives and says in a cynical voice 'Who sold you this then?', when they arrive at a check-in desk, or most crucially when they complain. Directors and boards cannot directly control these moments of truth. Organizations have thousands, even millions, of them every day. Some will be good. Many will be bad. Customers will talk about the bad ones on average to some twelve other people, and so the negative perception of the organization spreads.

How many moments of truth does your company have per day? How many are good? How many are bad? How do you find out as a director? Do you even know who your customers are? Why do they buy from you? How many approaches are repeat business (the cheapest and best way of selling and increasing margins)? Who are your competitors? How are they doing on the moments-of- truth front? Have you positioned yourself in the markets so that your customers see you as providing consistently 'good value for money'? How do you create such a perception in the customer's mind?

To do this well, it is essential for boards to realize that they should not, and cannot, control the day-to-day operations of their business. This comes as a shock to those directors whose mindset has them sitting at the top of the organization issuing orders that are obeyed with precision as they cascade down the organization. Organizational life has never been like that; the more levels of hierarchy there are, the less likely it is that orders will be obeyed in the way they were intended, even in the most obedient organization.

The reality of organizations is that the customer's perception is usually created by the 'customer-facing staff', often some of the lowest-down in the hierarchy. These people deliver the product or service and often actually speak with the customer. They, and the quality of their immediate supervision, create or destroy the reputation of the company regardless of its Mission, Vision and Values, and Ethics Statements, and regardless of all the advertising, public relations and other expensive hype.

The fact that these folk are customer-facing makes them the company's greatest asset. They can *learn* from the customers and so help the organization respond to their changing needs. Directors rarely speak with customers except in formal circumstances – at Annual General Meetings, or when dealing with major complaints or litigation. None of these circumstances is suitable for sustained learning as they tend to be adversarial, rather than cooperative, by nature. The directors are rarely in sensitive listening or problem-solving mode during these dealings.

Constructive listening and systematic problem-solving for the customer have become essential elements of the learning systems created by companies like British Airways, Unipart, Rover Cars and the AA's Roadside Services Division. Some of these were nationalized industries and bad performers which have moved from the bottom rank in customers' perceptions to become world-class providers in the space of a decade. In each company a major organizational and cultural breakthrough has happened: it is accepted that the main source of information about the performance of the product or service, and the quality of the organization behind them, is the organization's members, who are encouraged to monitor continuously the customers' perceptions and comments and to learn systematically from them. One of the requirements is that the customer-facing staff and their supervisors are able to flex small levels of discretion over the product's or service's presentation and delivery, to fit the customer's specific needs. If this is not possible then there has to be a rapid response mechanism involving managers, for quick decisions about a specific customer.

The focus on learning from the customer means a significant shift of operational power which has two major effects.

1. It opens up the possibility of continuous learning *with*, rather than just from, the customers. This makes the jobs of the customer-facing staff and supervisors more interesting, and so helps retain well-trained people and thus increase the organizations' experience base whilst reducing costs.

2. It changes the nature of managerial and directoral work. As the customer-facing work groups become more *self*-managing through devolution of some power to them, so the management is released to focus on ensuring that the technical, information and, most importantly, the people development systems are installed and maintained so that continuous learning can take place.

For boards of directors it means that they have less chance of reverting to their old managerial or professional roles, more chance of budgeting time for monitoring the external environment, for reflecting and debating the complex changes there, and more time, ultimately, for giving thoughtful direction and leadership.

Emotional Climate

Boards have a crucial role in creating and maintaining the Learning Organization. They wittingly or unwittingly create the *emotional* climate that determines whether or not it is acceptable to be seen to learn at work. This may sound simplistic. It is not. Staff watch directors very closely to see if their words and their actions are in synchronization. Like Doubting Thomases they will believe it only if they see it. If the directors' behaviours are out of synchronization with their words then they will believe the behaviours. They will scan the board's edicts and crosscheck them constantly for inconsistencies, then talk about them across the organization. A problem for boards is that such behavioural inconsistencies do not have to be large ones to create a big impact. The leverage put on them by the work force magnifies the problem, which is often then amplified again by the organization's rumour mill. As an example, the chief executive of a UK telecommunications company sent out a memo ordering all departments to reduce their overhead spend by twenty percent in twelve months. On the same day he employed another personal assistant. Guess which message the people paid attention to, and which went round the rumour mill fastest? This created a negative emotional climate for the overhead reduction programme across the whole organization.

The most depressing case I have come across is the sinking of the *Herald of Free Enterprise* off Zeebrugge. The evidence of the Sheen Inquiry[5] lists bad employment practices, undermanning, alcoholism, and a lack of communications and care between the operations folk and the directors. 193 people died when the ship sailed with its bow doors open into winter seas. Townsend's counsel said 'In the circumstances Townsend Car Ferries accepts that this casualty was caused by its own faults and the faults of its employees. It is right . . . that the company should take responsibility.' Amongst other penalties the company was made to pay £350,000 for the inquiry costs and £50,000 costs to the National Union of Seamen. There was great public anger against the company and a wish to see the directors charged with corporate manslaughter. This idea was dropped eventually because, although boardroom decisions and failures can in principle form the basis of manslaughter liability if they were reckless and a cause of death, under present law it is difficult to identify a single director who can be charged. The public have remained angry about this unsatisfactory situation, so in 1996 the British government announced that it is considering a new law of 'corporate killing' to make directors more liable.

However, in the UK a precedent has already been set. In 1995 a corporate manslaughter case was successfully brought against a director and the legal precedent set. Whereas before it was considered too difficult to bring criminal charges against one or more directors for gross negligence, the prosecution of OLL (formerly Active Learning & Leisure), which ran an activity centre and was accused of being responsible for the deaths of four young canoeists in Lyme Bay, saw the subsequent fining for £60,000 and the jailing of the managing director, Peter Kite, for three years. This has helped change boards' views of corporate manslaughter. The UK Law Commission is looking at ways of making it easier to bring corporate manslaughter charges and will report in 1996.

If you look at all the recent UK disasters for which there has been a public enquiry, or a coroner's court – the Kings Cross Fire, the Clapham Rail Disaster (where British Rail were fined £250,000), the *Marchioness* disaster, the Hillsborough tragedy, the Cowden rail disaster – one key point stands out from the judges' or coroners' remarks in all cases: the information needed to avoid the disaster was known somewhere inside the organization but neither the system nor the emotional climate existed to move that information easily to where it was needed.

The emotional climate created by the board is crucial. Much of the present outrage about directors' high pay, benefits, pensions, stock options and 'performance-related' pay schemes is not about the rates of pay *per se* but more that these rewards are being self-awarded without any apparent relation to the enterprise's performance, while ninety-nine percent of the company is getting tiny or no pay increases and the shareholders are not seeing any added value. Many directors do not seem to have any idea of the powerful emotionally negative messages they are giving to the owners and the work force, or the effect this has on the emotional climate, and hence the energy and productivity, of their organization.

We like to think of our organizations as calm, rational, logical places. They are not. They are prone to the full range of human emotions. Managers are there to install and maintain the systems which monitor and control the daily operations, and rightly so. The directors are there to ensure that at the *centre* of the enterprise, not the top, there is a heart and brain. This 'heart' of the business creates an emotional temperature appropriate to that specific organization. This is the essence of the organization's climate or 'culture'. It is

the board that ultimately determines this culture, but few understand this, or accept it, or know what to do about it.

Learning from Mistakes

A key part of learning is in making mistakes. Recent work in Germany[6] shows that an overconcentration on *not* making mistakes,
through breaking down the job into very simple components, actually
increases the rate of error. People learn how not to make mistakes by
being in a climate where they are stretched by taking on a little too
much and then have to grapple with the consequences. If they break
the job down into portions they can handle rather than having it
imposed upon them from above, they are more likely to succeed.

How are mistakes handled in your organization? In most, the
idea of publicly admitting your mistakes is seen as corporate suicide,
or at best career limiting. When they make a mistake, people do
what they have learned to do since they left the cradle – they cover
up.

One of the great lies of organizational folklore is 'I'm from head
office, I'm here to help you'. Everyone 'knows' that that person is
really here to blame the innocent, promote the guilty, and bayonet
the wounded – so we cover up.

Creating the Climate for Learning

Creating a Learning Organization does not require a huge investment of time or money. You can make a strong case that without
such learning one is wasting both. If you look at the two figures
for the Operational Learning Cycle below, you will see that it
requires only two questions to get into constructive problem-solving
mode. It is in the Non-Learning Organization that four questions
are required, and where the energy is diverted into hiding the truth
rather than doing something about it. The Non-Learning Organization abuses the energies of its people.

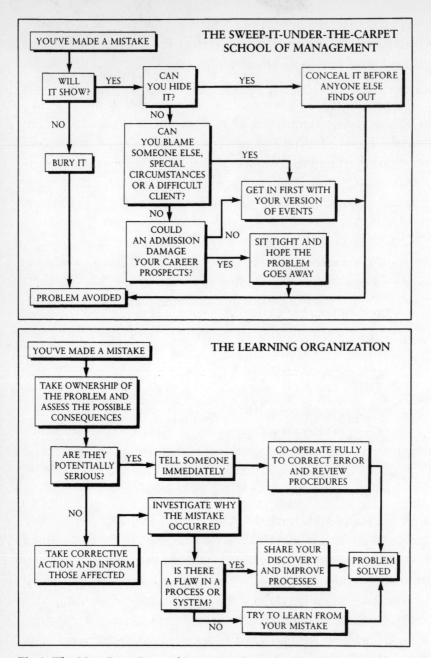

Fig 1 The Non-Learning and Learning Organization: Operational cycle
Source: Keith Grint, Templeton College, Oxford

At its simplest and most cost-effective, the Learning Organization requires each director and manager at the beginning or end of the day to spend ten minutes with his or her direct reports asking, 'What went right?', 'What went wrong?', 'What can we do about it?' and 'Who else needs to know?'. These questions are geared to *continuously* striving to learn, to improve what the customer actually experiences (organizational effectiveness), and show the managers and accountants what they need to strive for through the efficient use of scarce resources to achieve this (organizational efficiency).

Four Conditions

A Learning Organization requires the board to commit to and act upon four conditions:

1. That each member of the organization is encouraged to learn regularly and rigorously from their daily work, and to ensure that time is budgeted for this.
2. That there are systems in place to capture that learning, celebrate and reward it, and move it to where it is needed.
3. That the organization is encouraged by its owners and directors to transform itself continuously through its internal and external learning processes.
4. That such learning is valued in the appraisal and reward systems, and in the asset base of the organization.

A good example of a company taking this approach over the last few years is the very successful Chaparral Steel in the USA. It has focused the whole of its work force on developmental projects. Virtually everyone is involved in a project aimed at either improving present processes or developing new ones. Chaparral is outstanding in its *systematic* selection of projects for improvement or development. It monitors regularly and rigorously, and then ensures that what is learned on one project is carefully applied to others. It is rigorous on its *learning audit* – on what could be done more, what could be done less, what is satisfactory. This auditing can also lead, at the strategic level, into creating asset value through the creation of a legal right over the learning – the 'intellectual property'.

I have also been involved in the handing-on of learning from one project to another with BP Exploration (BPX) and its 'Stuck Pipe' project. When a drilling pipe sticks it loses a lot of exploration time and that costs a lot of money. So BPX was careful in ensuring that the learning on one project was captured and passed on in a user-friendly way to other BP explorations. For a very small investment BPX thinks that it has saved tens of millions of dollars a year.

In contrast, I once worked with a manufacturer of turbines, magnificent pieces of engineering which were hand-crafted to incredibly small tolerances. They were so delicately balanced that their transportation and installation were art forms in themselves. A 'set' was installed successfully on a customer's site and all went well for the first six months until one night a cleaner put her water-loaded bucket on a convenient lever. The lever had no safety catch and the weight of the bucket slowly opened a water valve. When the fast-spinning blades hit the rising water level the turbine shredded itself. The cost of the damage was enormous, in terms of both direct and consequential loss. It was painstakingly rebuilt over two years and reinstalled. Then the same accident, with the same cleaner, happened again. No-one had told the cleaner of the consequences of her action, and no-one had taken responsibility for redesigning the lever. Nothing had been learned. Again the direct and indirect costs were huge and this time heads rolled – but, interestingly, not the cleaner's. She was seen as the least culpable. No-one had installed a learning audit at any level.

Mistakes and Recognition

Another way in which a non-learning climate can block the ability to learn is by not giving people recognition for their work. Even in organizations that swallow up any individuality, the basic human need to be recognized as a personality will always show itself. Ideally people get it from their boss and peers for a job well done, but most bosses do not seem to work that way. They are often peculiarly reluctant to say a simple 'thanks'. If people are never thanked, they will opt for 'negative recognition' rather than have no recognition at all. They will purposely make mistakes or not comply. Making a mistake consciously, maliciously or just sloppily at least gets you recognized, even if the emotional climate of negative criticism and punishment is dreadful. This kind of non-learning climate is, sadly, widespread.

THE BOARD'S ROLE IN THE LEARNING ORGANIZATION

There is a simple three-level hierarchy in organizations which the Chinese have used for some 5,000 years, and the Greeks (whose words we still use in English) evolved some 3,500 years ago:

Policy
Strategy
Tactics/Operations

Policy and strategy are the worlds of the board and directors. The remaining ninety-nine percent of the people in the organization will spend their lives in the operations loops of learning, dealing tactically with the immediate problems of crises and deviations from plans. This is both necessary and sufficient for work groups, but it should not preclude them from having an input on policy and strategy. They too are living in the changing outside world and may well have good information or ideas for the board on how to help redirect the business to keep it alive within its energy niches.

Taking the three-level hierarchy of policy, strategy, and operations, one can overlay a figure-of-eight, or double-loop, of learning over the hierarchy which puts the board at the *centre* of the learning cycles, not at the top of the organization. The *Learning Board* should be the central processor for the two cycles of organizational learning – operational (day-to-day) and policy/strategic (long-term).

In the operations loop of learning the customer-facing staff, supervisors, managers and support staff are charged with listening carefully to the external and internal customers and then creating and improving systems of product or service delivery which are effective from the customer's point of view. Once the customer is convinced of your promises about 'good value for money', then you can set *effectiveness levels* of performance for your staff to aspire to before you begin to focus on organizational efficiency – whilst ensuring you always keep that public perception of effectiveness firmly in the customer's sight. 'Bottom-line' fixation to the exclusion of customers' concerns looks wonderful to the accountants in the short term, but tends quickly to create a non-learning organization. It is a very good way of losing everyone's job in the long term.

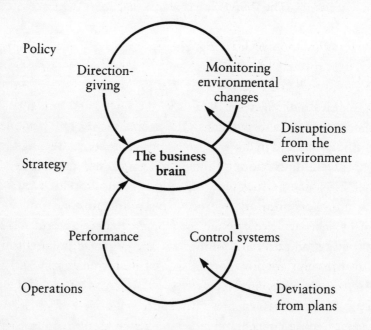

Figure 2 The Double Loop of Learning, part i

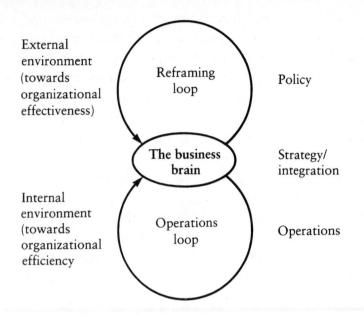

Figure 3   The Double Loop of Learning, part ii

In the policy loop of learning, the directors are both listening to what operations tell them is going on, and simultaneously monitoring the complexity and chaos of the continual changes in those external environments which create their ecological niches for their enterprise – the levels outside of which the organization will die. These levels must be monitored in the following environments: political, physical environmental, economic, social, technological and trade. The dynamic balances struck here by the board are crucial to the effectiveness of the organization in relation to the outside world.

It is the board's role to ensure that the dynamic balance is kept between organizational effectiveness and organizational efficiency. When the chips are down, it is usually better to maintain customer-perceived organizational effectiveness at all costs, provided the cash keeps flowing, rather than internally-perceived organizational efficiency, since concentration on efficiency alone usually leads to corporate collapse in the medium term.

This is an unfashionable statement in the Anglo-Saxon business world because of the present fixation on 'bottom lines', 'quarterly results', 'rapid increases in shareholder value' and other often ill-applied notions which involve overanalysing, and then slimming down, an enterprise to the point of collapse. Digging up a plant to examine its roots with ever-increasing frequency is a sure way of killing it. Organizations, like plants, need time to bed down (stability), fertilizing (strategic thinking), and relatively fallow periods (continuity).

Let me give two examples of how a fixation on efficiency, coupled with a lack of imagination and vision, created havoc.

The first is a retail bank. The customers saw it as a friendly place and were very loyal, so there was less of the customer 'churn' that their competitors faced. Moreover, a number of their customers were the first in their social class who were likely to have significant wealth to pass on to the next generation. The only financial services company they really knew and trusted was this bank. Logically, the bank was set up well to expand through its carefully nurtured customer-friendly and 'trusted advisor' perception developed over one hundred years.

But the top executives were changed and the newcomers decided the bank needed restructuring and that the old-guard managers were not up to scratch. So they sacked many of them and brought in a new group of directors and managers who were not happy with the bank's old external image, despite the customer-satisfaction level. They were caught up in the 'new industry formula' of having to provide 'a full range of financial services'. New logos, Vision and Mission Statements were promulgated and the whole internal structure of the bank was changed to ensure a massive reduction in costs. They dramatically reduced staff, managers' discretionary ability and customer contact. They started to charge for customer services which before had been seen as important for the customer-friendly image.

This all had a beneficial effect on the bottom line in the short term. The accountants and directors were happy and they talked much of increasing shareholder value. However, they lost over fifteen percent of their customers in two years – a devastating hit for any business.

The customers left not because any other retail bank was offering better or cheaper services but mainly because the new boards and senior managers had created a negative, efficiency-only focused, customer-unfriendly emotional climate. The 'moments of truth' had switched from being mainly positive to mainly negative. This soured quickly the many years of careful internal investment in customer relations.

Now they are seen by most as 'just another bank' and have to fight for their range of investment-orientated services just like their competitors, whereas under the old climate the customers would have asked for such help automatically. The bright young red-braced 'Gordon Gecko'-like men, not women, who went for the bottom-line-only approach have all been sacked. But the customers no longer trust the bank enough to give easy, profitable repeat business. The long-term effectiveness of the business has been severely compromised.

My second example is a telecommunications company that was installing a state-of-the-art coin-phone system nationally. There were increasing complaints from the public about its performance, specifically that most seemed to be out of order and signalling 'emergency calls only'. At first the board paid little attention to such complaints and put them down to a combination of the system taking time to settle in and the tendency for customers to complain anyway. Little hard data was requested. Then the national newspapers picked up the story and ran with it. Internal investigations started.

It emerged that the company was a very obedient one and had orders from the top to reduce the overhead spend by twenty percent in twelve months. The coin-phone division managers were not happy. They were not even sure what an 'overhead spend' was, so to make sure they were doing the right thing they reduced the total budget spend by twenty percent in a year. Whereas some divisions were vastly overstaffed and could easily reduce their spend in this way without affecting effectiveness, the coin-phone folk were already understaffed. The original reason why the phones were not working was that there were not enough people to go around and empty the coins out. The reductions made things much worse. Apparent short-term efficiency through dramatically reduced costs had been gained at the expense of a total loss of the effectiveness of the system and the goodwill of the customers.

The board finally responded to the barbs of bitter press criticism by throwing a lot of money at the problem until they achieved some 99.8 percent effectiveness daily for the system nationwide. Then they used 'Action Learning Groups' of staff from all levels of the division to keep that level of effectiveness whilst they moved into the efficiency cycle of learning. They now have a world-class coin-phone system, have outsourced the coin collection to a security firm, and have gained an awful lot of learning about specifying the effectiveness *and* efficiency levels of cost-reduction programmes before they start. This has been passed on to other projects.

The Board as the Business Brain

The board sits at the intersection of the organizational effectiveness and efficiency cycles as the centre of the *business brain*, taking a 'helicopter view' of policy and strategy issues. In Figures 2 and 3 I have deliberately drawn the two major learning cycles of the enterprise, policy and operations, as *overlapping* the central processing function – the strategy level – to symbolize the business brain – the idea that the learning comes not just from the directors but from *all* members of the organization and from those outside it. The information and wisdom of all 'stakeholders' in and around an organization is a valuable commodity which directors need to appreciate and use.

The UK has pioneered work on organizational learning for some thirty years. One of the most carefully evaluated pieces of social research is the Hospitals Internal Communications Project for the UK National Health Service.[7] (Ironically, the NHS is now going through its own overemphasis on efficiency at the cost of effectiveness measured in terms of health gain.) The definitive HIC Project research by Reg Revans in the hospitals, based on 'Action Learning

Groups' – small numbers of cross-disciplinary and multi-level members who take responsibility for both analysing *and* implementing the learning gained from addressing key organizational issues – opened the way for many different types of projects both in the public sector and in industry.

Since the mid-1970s, a template for the four conditions for a Learning Organization has been developed by such companies as The General Electric Company of the UK, British Airways, Rover Cars, ICL Fujitsu and Unipart, all of whom try to place *learning* as central to developing business effectiveness and efficiency. They are realizing that this is not just a bottom-line issue but also a balance-sheet issue. Such learning can now be turned into legal property through the creation of 'Intellectual Property Rights' which can then be valued on the balance sheet (see later).

A central idea of the 'business brain' is that it is the focus and locus of the *organization's* debate about learning. It is where key organizational issues are identified, ideas generated imaginatively, and people given responsibility to go away to both tackle the problems and implement solutions in such a way that others can learn from them. This is too much for any board to do alone so it must rely on the goodwill and enthusiasm of its people to do this. It is here that an enterprise gets the energy to drive itself forward. This brings us back to the quality of the emotional climate that the board creates throughout their organization.

Measuring the Climate of Learning

In order to create a climate of learning, one needs first to benchmark where the organization is now on a number of key issues. I have developed my own Organizational Climate Survey instrument which looks at ten organizational dimensions, as shown below. I take a sample across the company and ask people where they are, and where they want to be, on each dimension.

Adaptability
Work quality
Level of personal responsibility
Financial rewards
Non-financial rewards
Organizational clarity
Individual performance indicators
Group performance indicators
Learning climate
Quality of leadership

Using both statistical and qualitative analysis, key problems can be identified at all levels of the organization. People can then be brought together in 'action learning' mode to take responsibility for analysing and implementing solutions to them, thus correcting the enterprise through the members themselves.

There are many ways of creating this *debating and learning climate*. General Electric in the USA has developed 'Town Meetings' where the management face a mass meeting of staff and work together on identifying the issues they all believe they should be working on. They then debate the issues identified and agree Action Learning Groups who report back to further mass meetings before and during implementation. Chaparral Steel also uses project groups to refine its organizational learning. Indeed, many organizations are beginning to call on staff knowledge and energy to analyse, debate and implement solutions in real time as the trend towards 'delayered' organizations means that there are no spare people to call on. The work force have to think and implement these thoughts for themselves, and learn from their experiences.

Four Tasks

The members of the board need to take the ideas about learning and apply them to themselves. They need to look at their board structure and ensure that it is designed to cope with the four Dilemmas and the four *Tasks* of the board that derive from them – Policy Formulation, Strategic Thinking, Supervision of Management, and Accountability. This means creating a structure which allows time for thinking strategically *as well as* proper stewardship of the enterprise.

As organizations begin the long haul towards more self-management at the operations level,* the board is increasingly free to address itself to the four Tasks of the board. The problem is that the structure of most boards is not conducive to debate, learning, adaptation and continuous development. Most are structured in a legally-orientated, administrative and developmentally-blocking manner.

A review of the structures typically found around the world shows why:

THE NON-EXECUTIVE BOARD

Here the board wholly comprises non-executive directors, notionally independent, who decide policy and strategy which they then delegate to the chief executive to execute whilst keeping the ultimate direction-giving responsibilities and liabilities to themselves. This often distances the board from the realities of operations, particularly when the chief executive is not a full member of the board. Even when he or she is, another problem arises. If the CEO is the only executive present then they have enormous

---

* See, for example, Krystyna Weinstein's book, *Action Learning*, HarperCollins 1995.

power in the business as they control information both to and from the board. This can cause a very unhealthy situation which if it lasts for any time can corrupt the whole. As Jack Welch said when describing his takeover of General Electric in the USA, 'it had become an organization with its face towards the CEO and its ass towards the customer!'

This type of board is often found in the USA, sometimes linked to a two-tier board, and, I think, goes a long way towards explaining the annoyance of many shareholders at the highly-personalized CEO power and lack of constructive criticism witihin the board. This type of board is also common in New Zealand, where the non-executive role is treated very positively and has become a career in itself. It is also often found around the world on public or semi-public service boards where an element of independent disinterest is needed.

THE EXECUTIVE BOARD

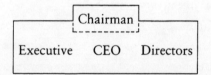

This is the most common type of board, found in family companies, owner-directed businesses and the subsidiaries of multi- and trans-national companies around the world. Although strong on knowing what is happening inside the business, it is usually weak on monitoring the outside world. It suffers an obvious lack of diversity, criticism and debate. It has a propensity to clone its membership, its assumptions and its style of thinking. Usually the CEO is dominant and may well take the chairman's role as well. If there is an outside chairman, his or her relationship with the board can be very difficult as the CEO is everyone else's boss, so debating and questioning by the chairman can lead to him or her being excluded by the executive directors who want to maintain their political relationship with the CEO.

THE TWO-TIER BOARD, OR 'SENATE' BOARD

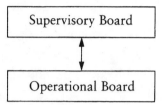

This is seen commonly in such countries as Germany, the Netherlands and France. It has been proposed as a universal model for boards in the European Union. It has an upper board which deals with the strategic issues and a lower board which represents the different interests in the company, particularly the trades unions. The supervisory board is charged with informing the operational board of its broad intentions in the medium and long term and receiving the performance figures from the operational board. Although theoretically a strong structure, the two-tier, or Senate-style, board performance has not lived up to expectations, particularly in Germany and France where it is under critical pressure for two reasons. First, the disinterestedness of the supervisory board can be compromised easily if each 'independent' board member is really a representative of interlocked shareholders and bankers, which is often the case. Second, it is easy for both boards to descend into party politics at regional or national level, or into the micro-politics of the organization and its personalities. There is then a tendency to exclude the other board, in which case both boards lose sight of working towards a common end.

THE UNITARY BOARD

> Independent Directors
> Chairman
> Chief Executive
> Executive Directors

This is the classic 'Anglo-Saxon' model found across the United Kingdom and in many parts of the Commonwealth. It assumes, backed by law, that all directors are equal and must accept the same responsibilities and liabilities for the performance of the enterprise. It assumes that the executive directors, led by the chief executive or managing director, are responsible for the *supervision* of the operational side of the business and for agreeing and executing the strategies, whilst the independent, non-executive directors add value by forming policy and ensuring accountability whilst helping the board debate with, and criticize constructively, the executives' actions and performance. Such independent directors are crucial to both the 'Performance' and 'Conformance' of the unitary board so that the interests of shareholders and other stakeholders are heard and protected.

It has obvious drawbacks, particularly as so much depends on the true independence at board level of *both* the executive *and* the independent directors. This means that their selection, training to competence, appraisal and removal are key issues for all stakeholders. In turn this means that performance criteria need to be agreed and systems installed by all the directors and then maintained by the chairman.

Training an executive director to independence of thought at board level is difficult – but not impossible. However, of the board models I have seen around the world, the unitary board has the best potential for being self-correcting, for addressing the four Directoral Dilemmas, and for keeping the ecological balances of a business. I predict a strong convergence towards a unitary board approach in the present debate in Germany, France and even possibly Japan.

It is the model on which I base the rest of this book.

Deriving the Model of the Learning Board

A long accepted model of the unitary board has been:

E X T E R N A L	*Accountability* Reporting to shareholders Ensuring statutes and regulatory compliance Reviewing audit reports	*Strategic thinking* Reviewing and initiating strategic analysis Formulating strategy Setting corporate direction
	Appointing and rewarding chief executive	
I N T E R N A L	*Supervision* Reviewing key executive performance Reviewing business results Monitoring budgetary control and corrective actions	*Corporate policy* Approving budgets Determining compensation policy for senior executives Creating corporate culture
	SHORT-TERM	LONG-TERM

Figure 4 Bob Tricker's early model of a board's roles [8]

This model has been an important building block for my Learning Board model. It demonstrates clearly the four Tasks and the need for sufficient diversity within the board if it is to cope with the intellectual and operational challenges which the four Directoral Dilemmas pose. Board members must *between them* be able to cope with the short-term and long-term, the organizational effectiveness (external) and organizational efficiency (internal) issues simultaneously. This is not an easy capability to develop and this requirement is often rejected outright by successful 'hands-on' managers who have not been inducted or included into directoral competence.

However, I have two problems with this 'traditional' board model.

First, I think that strategy and policy are positioned wrongly on it and need reversing on the right hand side. If we go back to the original Greek meaning of 'policy' and follow its entry into the English language as 'polity', then we see that it relates to dealings in, and with, the political world. I think that this captures the externally-orientated, long-term style of thinking described by the top right hand quadrant. 'Strategy' in the original Greek refers to the world of the military generals where, once the policy is agreed, one works out how to position oneself to achieve the political will, or purpose, given the broad deployment of the scarce resources available.

In an imagined Greek example, if the policy is to attack Thrace because they have been stealing our land and insulting our women, then it is the generals (strategists) who say 'Great idea, and we know how to deliver it, but there are some problems ... Do you remember the little local difficulties we had last year down in Thermopylae? We lost one army altogether, and the trireme development programme is running three years late, so even if we needed them we cannot rely on the navy. What we really want is more time and money to get the logistics together to deliver your policy.' Policy is about political will, or purpose. Strategy is about the broad deployment of resources to achieve this.

The second problem I have is that the central activity of the board is to select and reward the chief executive. This serves no good purpose today. It helps explain the over-fixation of boards on their pay and conditions, but it does not forgive them for their greed.

My model of a Learning Board takes the same quadrant framework, transposes policy and strategy and places the process

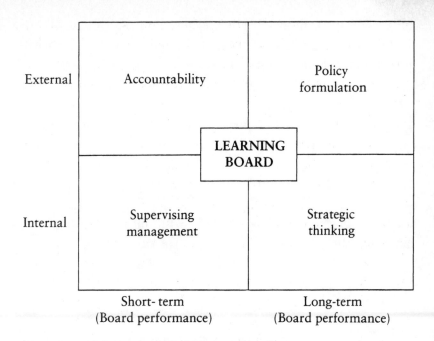

Figure 5   The simple Learning Board model

of learning as the pivot around which the board members revolve. This allows them to be the 'central processor' of the organization whilst allowing all parts of the enterprise to learn simultaneously to survive – bringing us back to the $L \geq C$ axiom.

The Learning Board is the centre of the Learning Organization's 'business brain'. This model allows for a clearer understanding of the tasks of the board, who should take the leading roles, and when.

There are two sides to a Learning Board: *Conformance* and *Performance*. 'Conformance' involves two aspects: Accountability (conformance to legislation, regulation, shareholder and stakeholder wishes and audits) and Supervision of Management (conformance to key performance indicators, cashflow, budgets and projects). 'Performance' involves Policy Formulation and Strategic Thinking, which drive the whole enterprise forward allowing it to survive and grow by maintaining and developing its position in its energy niches.

So the detailed model of the Learning Board is shown in Figure 6 (opposite).

All the four board Tasks – Policy Formulation, Strategic Thinking, Supervision of Management and Accountability – feed naturally into each other as elements of an annual cycle of the board's learning. This can come as a shock to directors more used to board meetings being driven by a company secretarial legal and administrative agenda, plus the usual micro-political infighting. This is not to knock company secretaries. They are a much maligned group and have a necessary job reporting to the chairman on the preparation of board agendas and ensuring that a board fulfils its statutory duties to the company, the legislators, the regulators, and the stakeholders.

The Natural Rhythm of the Board's Year

The effectiveness of the Learning Board depends on the understanding that there should be a natural *rhythm* to a board's year. Board meetings are not just a set of regular, or arbitrary, comings-together on a set agenda for confrontations between the chairman and chief executive, or the independent and executive directors. Nor are they a way of structuring a few hours with a good lunch to ensure that the members do not feel too embarrassed at picking up their directors' fees. There is serious work to be done in each of the four quadrants, and this work has a logical sequence.

The natural rhythm of the board starts at the beginning of the enterprise's financial year with an annual *Review of Policy*. This has the whole board reflecting upon the changing world in relation to the board's espoused purpose, vision and values, culture, and external environment monitoring systems.

This should lead at the minimum to a six-monthly *Review of Strategic Thinking*, where policy is used as the coordinates for exploring the changing political, physical, economic, social, technological and trade environments so that business, financial, and people strategies can be derived from them.

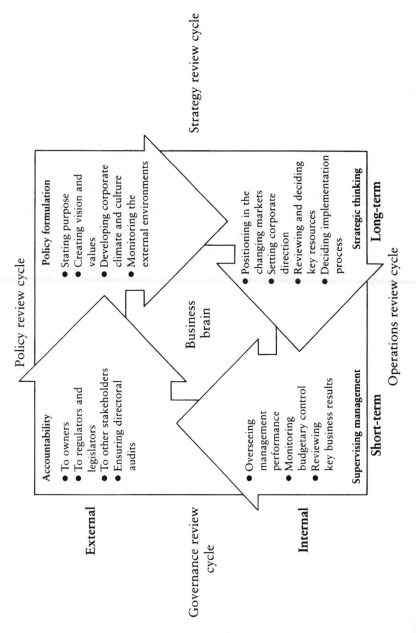

Figure 6   The full Learning Board model

This is checked and learned from through a monthly *Review of the Supervision of Management* where the key performance indicators, budget, cashflow and project management positions are checked. This is *not* done in detail by the board. The board is looking for the changes in patterns and trendlines compared with their strategies. If detailed investigations are needed this is done outside the board through the executives and the results are reported back. A major problem here is that we all think we know better than the present managers how to do their jobs and so will get bogged down in detail if the chairman gives us any chance.

The annual cycle of the board ends with the careful checking of their *Accountability* at least three months before the end of their financial year. This process ensures that the board is legally and emotionally in synchronization with the needs of the company itself, the shareholders, legislators and regulators, customers, staff, suppliers, the physical environment and local communities.

Directors' Roles

One can immediately sense whether a board is a conformance-orientated or performance-orientated type. A deeper question is whether they do this consciously or unconsciously. Do the directors position themselves and budget their time so that they can learn continuously from actions and feedback? What roles should the executive and independent directors take to ensure such continuous learning? There are many ways of dividing up the combinations of short- and long-term thinking and internal and external orientations amongst directors; none is right for all occasions. It is up to the chairman to ensure that such division of labour is effective.

One way is for the independent directors to be focused on the policy role with the executive directors focusing on the conformance aspects of accountability and supervision of management. Strategy is agreed by both types of director.

Other boards will say this is not correct and focus their independent directors on the external aspects of policy and accountability, leaving the executive directors to deal with the internal aspects of strategy and supervision of management. I think that this is also a very useful working definition for the basic definition of responsibilities of the chairman (policy and accountability) and the chief executive (strategy and supervision of management).

But it is not the only possibility. Given the growing diversity of many boards it is not wise to be too prescriptive here as the best split of the roles and responsibilities depends on the combination of personalities and capabilities at the time. What is important is that a board fully addresses the issues of 'who does what': where scarce resources are best deployed at board level, and whether the chairman and chief executive's roles are explicit to both the board and the stakeholders.

I have noted in my work that the biggest problems seem to arise if the dividing line between independent and executive directors is

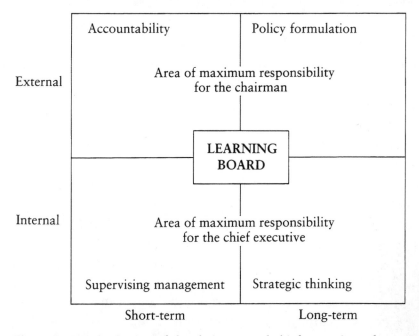

Figure 7 Simple sharing of the chairman and chief executive roles

drawn diagonally from top left to bottom right of the Learning model. Here the chairman is definitely responsible for policy and the chief executive for supervision of management, but there is every possibility for confusion and argument about strategy and accountability unless there is a highly robust process by which the directors debate and reach consensus. Such a process is rarely well-developed and so turf wars break out between the two types of director.

Similarly, a line drawn top right to bottom left often leaves the chairman clearly responsible for accountability (which is the law in many countries), and the CEO for strategic thinking. But it also means that policy and supervision of management are likely to be contentious. In theory, sharing these two between all directors leads to solutions of the highest common factor. My observation is that they more often fall into the lowest common denominator trap.

A better approach is for the board as a whole to design the main focus of their responsibilities collectively as simply *directors*, to allocate leadership appropriately, based on the individuals available, and to review the outcomes of these decisions at least annually as part of the corporate governance audit process.

To reinforce the well-known Law of Human Cussedness, I know of a number of major international companies and family firms where the chairman and chief executive roles are transposed. The titles are kept but they take on the opposite role. Again, provided this is clear to all players it can work, although annual general meetings can be a bit puzzling for shareholders. It is only when both fight for a single role, usually that of chief executive, and abandon the other role entirely that trouble starts.

The annual rhythm of the board specified above is a rather mechanistic approach – a planned series of 'awaydays' for the board to write in their diaries at the beginning of a financial year and to which all are committed to attend as their highest priority. If you adopt even such a mechanistic process you will be in the top quartile of effective boards and starting the long climb to becoming both a performing and a conforming Learning Board.

Independent and executive directors around the world have responded with universal enthusiasm to the ideas of the Learning Board – to both the model and the natural rhythm for the board; but many directors have had a tough time facing up to their seemingly ambiguous roles under the four Directoral Dilemmas. They find it difficult to come to terms with the idea that even an executive director has an independent and equal role to play within the board itself, particularly if those executives see themselves as mainly representing their function back in the operations side of the business.

Whilst this is understandable, it is not helpful. If they drop back into their old senior management roles they effectively stop giving direction. Many executive directors will admit that they are so functionally specialized that they cannot ask questions of the other executive or professional disciplines or make helpful comments. Therein lies a clue for the chairman.

Most independent directors say the same. They see themselves brought onto the board because of the different experience and outside connections they can bring with them. Again, they feel constrained, as any human being does, not to ask probing questions in case they should look rude, inexperienced, foolish or naive. This is understandable but not forgivable in a director. A director needs to use 'intelligent naivety' as a key tool of the job.

It is the chairman's role to see that proper induction, inclusion and training to competence is carried out for the board *as an effective working group*, and for each director on it.

The key point is that *independence of thought* is demanded of *all* directors when on a board. This requires that they use their 'naive intelligence' to advantage, pursue discriminating questions until they get a satisfactory answer that they and other board members understand, are not put off by the technobabble from other disciplines, and pursue the company's interests above all else. It is the chairman's role to ensure that this happens.

The role of the board and its directors in the twenty-first century will be more and more concerned with balancing internal and external issues in a rapidly changing world. Directoral competence – independence of imagination and thought, plus the nous to run an effective enterprise – will determine an organization's success. Directing is becoming a proper job in itself. It is each director's duty to ensure that he or she is trained for it.

PERFORMANCE ASPECTS OF THE BOARD

CHAPTER 3

Policy Formulation

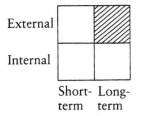

Organizational effectiveness: Long-term, externally-oriented thinking

Policy formulation is the least understood, and so least visited, aspect of directing. There are four major aspects of policy formulation: Purpose, Vision and Values, and Emotional Climate and Culture are 'soft aspects' (socio-emotional) and vital to the continued existence of the enterprise; Monitoring the External Environment is 'hard' (systems-structural). Most managers and professionals are much happier with the last.

It is the first three socio-emotional aspects that create the coordinates by which all other activities of the business operate. They are what create the organizational 'heart' that employees will (or will not) commit themselves to, thus providing the crucial 'corporate energy' needed to achieve the Purpose. Many directors do not recognize the importance of this, and so treat the organization as a logical machine which will immediately understand and obey orders through its systems and structure.

PURPOSE

What is the purpose of your enterprise? Why is it here? What is its reason for being? What must it do to ensure that it is relevant? How can it stay within its 'energy niches' to achieve its purpose?

For commercial enterprises the answer may seem glaringly obvious – to make a profit. However, in these competitive times such an answer is not good enough. Making a profit is a given: if you don't make a profit, your organization dies. So what is it that transcends profit and gives the business its true reason for being?

Most companies have difficulty saying why they are here. Even those that can are often embarrassingly anodyne in their wishes 'to be the best', 'to be the leading' in whatever field. These platitudes are duly built into the grandly and expensively produced 'Mission Statement' which adorns company reports, entrance lobbies, and offices throughout the business. But does anyone believe and commit to it? Usually not. The board's thinking and words are rarely understood, and as their words and actions are probably seen by the members not to be in synchronization anyway, the whole exercise is rapidly devalued. Looking at such statements dispassionately, of course everyone wants to be 'the best'. You can hardly say 'we strive to be number seven in this region in three years' time'; it just doesn't energize people. A company's stated Purpose should effectively position it in such a way that its people feel able to align their energies and direct them towards a common organizational purpose.

Some directors' views are that they were appointed to directorships as achievers and doers, not to sit around dealing with abstract and wimpish ideas like 'purpose', 'alignment' and 'attunement'. It takes time for them to understand that the members of their organization want to be given clear direction and the emotional climate and resources with which to get there. Some manager-directors only achieve this understanding on retirement when they have time to reflect – and that is a clue in itself.

I have already shown that the word 'policy' derives from the Greek and is concerned with the political world – macro and micro. The word 'political' is enough immediately to turn off many hard-headed senior mangers who have spent their lives trying to avoid politics and politicians. This is understandable in all parts of the world, but it is hardly realistic. Most try to avoid conflict with the political world as much as they can and then place two-way bets on the rest, hoping to gain some sort of certainty and even reward whichever way the political pendulum swings. Few are determined to place all their bets on a single political party because their objective is not the win/lose game but the win/win game of survival and growth. Even in Communist China where, although there is only one official party, there are plenty of factions to back. But the board has to position the company in all the political environments – party political, national and regional political, environmental (the 'green' issues), economic (national and international), social, technological and trade (the 'PPESTT' analysis) – and set up systems for monitoring the trends and changes in them.

A 'PPESTT' analysis provides the intellectual framework within which the board must decide its Purpose, striking the balances that ensure its continuing existence. This is not easy. Many businesses do not last long. Recent research has shown that the average life-to-death cycle of a *Fortune 500* company is just forty years and falling. And that is for very large corporations with built-in inertia. Facing up to, and learning from, the 'political' world is a fundamental of organizational survival and the board is central, but not exclusive, to it – many other parts of the organization can contribute.

The board has to define a Purpose to which all members of the organization can commit, and create an emotional climate within which all the stakeholders *want* to commit. This is the 'heart' of the enterprise.

What might such a Purpose look like? I have chosen five examples which have stood the test of a decade:

Glaxo

'Glaxo is an integrated research-based group of companies whose corporate purpose is to create, discover, develop, manu-facture and market throughout the world safe, effective medi-cines of the highest quality which will bring benefits to patients through improved longevity and quality of life, and to society through economic value.'

Pearson

'Pearson, a major international provider of media content, aims for distinctive products that deliver information, edu-cation, and entertainment in ways that people want them.'

Apple Computer

'Our goal has always been to create the world's friendliest, most understandable, most useable computers – computers that empower the individual.'

IBM

'We shall increase the pace of change. Market-driven quality is our aim. It means listening and responding more sensitively to our customers. It means eliminating defects and errors, speeding up all our processes, measuring everything we do against a common standard, and involving employees totally in our aims.'

Microsoft

'A personal computer on every desk and in every house.'

These words are all taken directly from their published literature. The words chosen and the length of the statement give a clear feel of the emotional climate of the organization.

I cannot tell you what your Purpose is; that is for your board to decide. A wise board will derive it in consultation with its staff, customers, suppliers and shareholders. I can warn that ending up with a simplistic 'biggest' or 'best' approach usually generates sniggers all round and induces downright hostility amongst the stakeholders, especially the staff and customers. Many organizations confuse the terms 'Mission', 'Vision' and 'Purpose'. I see 'Mission' as an achievable, managerial notion which forms a key part of the planning process. 'Purpose' and 'Vision' should *not* be easily achievable. They must be demanding or they will have little value. Reading some Mission Statements reminds me of the Oscar Wilde quotation: 'Anyone of sensibility cannot fail, on reading of the death of Little Nell, to laugh.' I know what he meant.

VISION AND VALUES

Vision

The corporate Vision is that big picture, far into the future, of what we will be like and feel like as we approach our Purpose. The Vision should be unattainable in the short and medium term, but sufficiently tantalizing for everyone to remain excited about it and see it as a real possibility, even in the worst of times.

Visions stretch our imaginations, ambitions, thoughts and behaviours to take us forward without any immediate expectation of short-term fulfilment such as that that comes from the operational work in hand. Visions are of a higher order. In China there is a classic symbol of the emperor, shown as a five-clawed dragon, always striving to clutch the flaming pink pearl of knowledge but never reaching it. I think of Vision in these terms – an invisible but energizing force that encourages people to attune, align and stretch out to generate the forward movement of the enterprise.

There are some circumstances in which Vision and Purpose can be one. Motorola's Vision is of a wire-less world in which everyone has a lifelong personal telephone number and a portable phone. A giant pharmaceuticals company has a Vision of becoming the world's first 'green' pharmaceutical company, built on environmentally friendly, natural products. Apple Computers has a Vision of a computer for every man, woman and child in America.

Such Visions are often built around what Gary Hamel and C. K. Prahalad have called 'core competencies' – key, closely related but generally applicable organizational competencies that embody the accumulated knowledge, attitudes and skills of the enterprise – its intellectual assets writ large.[9] Such core competencies are what allow a company to be a world leader in a particular ecological niche in their industry – 'on time delivery' at Federal Express; 'user friendliness' at Apple Computer; 'factory management' at Toyota, 'pocketability' at Sony; 'customer satisfaction' at British Airways.

Vision has a second important aspect. It 'reframes' the context in which staff, shareholders and stakeholders see their work 'today' and 'tomorrow'. Once the core competencies are clarified, the board can change their mindset to think of themselves as handling a portfolio of resources – knowledge, attitudes and skills – rather than just a collection of business units. They can then help the members of their company reframe their thinking about the competition and the outside world and so become more sensitive to their changing position in the competitive environment. Clarity of purpose has a positive impact on the intellectual quality of the board and consequently on senior management's Strategic Thinking.

Values

A Value is a belief in action, in this case an organizational, or corporate, belief. It says what is right and wrong, good or bad, for the organization, and thereby defines what will be rewarded or punished. Values shape organizational behaviour. Values must be backed up by actions or they will remain simply an aspiration.

Often board members see the definition of, and then living of, organizational values as an unproductive pursuit closely associated with 'social work' in the organization. But if the values on which an organization is built – typically 'excellence', 'honesty', 'quality', 'risk', 'innovation', 'creativity', 'reward', 'profit', 'competition', 'teamwork', 'probity' – are not seen to be acted out by their creators, the board, they will mean nothing.

There is an ethical base to the huge majority of enterprises. It is not possible to sustain long-term relationships with customers, staff, suppliers, legislators and shareholders without it. An unethical base can take you forward for some years, as the Schneider case in Germany, Daiwa case in the US, and Leeson case in Singapore demonstrate. But in the end there is always a reckoning-up to the detriment of all stakeholders.

What are the ethical values of your business? How do you determine what is right and wrong, good and bad in the way that your members handle relationships with others? What can they do and what can they not do within their jobs? It is easy to start listing such values as 'customer satisfaction', 'excellence', 'honesty' and so on, but do these reflect what your people actually *do*? How do you know? Are the values and behaviours tested regularly? As a board member do you occasionally telephone your organization's switchboard as a customer and try to buy your product or service? Have you tried to make a complaint and follow through what happens? Have you sat outside the factory on a Friday afternoon and inspected what is actually sent out to meet delivery targets? Have you worked on the night shift in the Accident and Emergency department of your hospital? Doing this can be an eye-opener and may show you that things are well out of line with the carefully crafted Value Statement which hangs on the office walls.

When I worked with one telecommunications company, the board perception of Values was so out of sync with the reality of operations that the chairman had to ensure that each board member, executive and independent, spent a day a week 'up poles or down holes' meeting the staff and customers, getting to grips with the reality of 'their' organization. Only after this consultative process was it possible to create a Value Statement to which the staff subscribed.

Value Statements provide an important reference point of the appraisal and reward systems of the organization. Once the Value Statement is articulated then it can be turned easily into a series of recognizable *behaviours* – he or she 'is seen to . . .'. This may sound obvious but seems to be rarely acted upon. When it is, it has a positive emotional effect on the enterprise. People can see that there is a Purpose and Vision, that there is a set of ethical values by which relationships within and without the organization will be conducted, and that they will be assessed and rewarded on these through the appraisal system.

I witnessed the power released by the acceptance of such an idea when I worked with a defence electronics company board. The company was an organizational mess having grown from 500 staff to some 5,000 in under two years on the back of two major contracts. They were a blend of civilian and military hardware, software and manufacturing folk based on four dispersed sites. There was little induction or inclusion, so people fell naturally into their old positions of comfort and behaved as if they were in their previous organization. On benchmarking I found some thirty-nine quite distinct corporate cultural climates, so the disorganization was debilitating. There was an obvious need to put business control systems in place and this was being done rapidly. Even so it was a year before the systems were working reasonably.

The Personnel Director and I decided to take a calculated risk with these hard-headed but demotivated people and pursue the Purpose, Vision and Values route quickly to get the majority of people roughly aligned and attuned. The board backed the idea, although, being engineers, most of them thought this a 'soft' approach. However, at that time anything that looked as though it might reduce the chaos was welcomed.

We started with the board working on the Purpose, Vision and Values Statements, and then used the fact that it was at that time a very rumour-based culture to allow controlled 'leaks' of the board's thinking. At this stage people preferred to believe the rumours rather than the formal announcements. But inevitably they began to ask, 'Why are we not being consulted?'

Once these questions became sufficiently intense, the Chief Executive addressed a mass meeting on each site and consulted people on the Purpose and Vision Statements. Consensus was achieved remarkably easily, as expected, so a key stage of alignment was reached. Then he challenged the audience to say what values and consequent behaviours should support such a Purpose and Vision, making it very clear that whatever was agreed would be taken into the operational cycle to form the basis of the appraisal and reward system. He asked for volunteers to form an action learning group to derive the values and behaviours.

People were excited by both ideas: the Purpose and Vision, which would give them an agreed direction, and the invitation to contribute to the action learning groups to derive their own appraisal and rewards system. They accepted that 50 percent of the assessment would hinge on the technical/project side of their work, but were intrigued by the idea that the other 50 percent would be based on *how* they reached the technical end. Some were downright cynical and went off to see the four trades unions represented on each site. We stressed that the behavioural assessment on the Values side would be exactly the same for the chairman and chief executive as for a part-time security guard. This was received with great interest but some scepticism.

The process led to a lot of discussion: amongst the work groups, with the action learning groups as the focus of the debate, and finally back in the mass site meetings. Within two months, eighteen key behaviours were agreed as the basis of the appraisal and reward system. The trades unions announced that they had, despite previous threatening noises, no objections to the behaviours or the appraisal process – in fact they said it seemed the clearest and fairest they had seen.

Significantly, people were asking for 'their' appraisal system to be implemented 'now'. They were desperate to know how they were doing amidst the chaos, and needed to have an agreed basis on which to talk with their bosses, colleagues and direct reports. So it was implemented rapidly with an agreed feedback procedure to upgrade the learning as it bedded down.

It has worked well for nine years with only minor modifications. Most importantly, it has ensured that induction and inclusion processes are treated seriously, as they form the basis from which the appraisal starts.

EMOTIONAL CLIMATE AND CULTURE

By now it should be obvious that the 'emotional' side of policy is not a soft option. Whether or not the members of an organization understand its direction and put their energy behind achieving the tasks needed to reach the enterprise's Purpose depends on its socio-emotional climate and culture.

A lot of directors I know feel a bit like Goering – 'When I hear the word culture I reach for my revolver.' But it is not yet another short-term management consultants' fad into which you will be encouraged to put a lot of money for little return. Creating an appropriate organizational culture is a fundamental building block of a healthy organization, and it is *measurable* – by parametric and non-parametric statistics, and other quantitative and qualitative methods.

A wise company is already measuring dimensions such as service satisfaction and product quality levels with its customers, so why not adopt a similar approach with staff? If retention of customers is a key to increased profitability, retention of key people, their experience and developing personal capabilities, is the best way of retaining customers.

Attunement

'Attunement', essential to energizing the forward drive of the organ-ization, is generated ultimately by the board. Organizational culture is defined broadly by how power is used and what will be rewarded and punished. This may be a crude definition of culture but it is a powerful one: you have been selected for your job because you are seen as technically competent in your previous job, have potential to develop, and look as though you will fit in to the culture of the new organization. As soon as you start someone will say, 'Oh! We don't do things like that around here.' You have hit the first signs of the corporate culture. 'How we do things around here' is a powerful bond. What do you do next? Do you adapt to it, knowing that you are doing something which is then less effective for the organization, or do you try to demonstrate the superiority of your methods and try to change the culture? These are difficult decisions for an incomer and can prejudice, unfairly, their inclusion process, either in the short term or for a long time. But culture is a tough beast with a long history.

The most useful description I know of culture is Clifford Geertz's: 'An historically transmitted pattern of meaning embodied in sym-bols; a system of inherited conceptions expressed in symbolic forms by means of which men communicate, perpetuate, and develop their knowledge about and attitudes towards life ... Man is an animal suspended in webs of signification he himself has spun. I take culture to be those webs, and the analysis of it to be therefore not an experimental science in search of law, but an interpretive one in search of meaning'.[10]

Organizations have histories, folktales, dramas, rituals, and rou-tines. The board should act as a true 'entrepreneur' – the stager of dramas – if it understands this and aligns the energies generated by its people to achieve its Purpose. The board are the main spinners of 'webs of signification'. To a great extent the board writes the official history of the company, tells its sagas to the outside world, creates its symbols and ceremonies (wittingly or otherwise), gives power to those they deem important, creates the 'class structure' of the enterprise, defines its enemies and the ethics of 'the way things are done around here'. The board's words and actions are watched carefully by the staff for changes in cultural priorities and the consequent power, reward and punishment systems. In their own interests they will follow the board's behaviour rather than their words. Understanding the importance of this allows for more effective organizational change.

As an example, I have been working with a financial services group in the West of England. They were undergoing massive changes and the board was trying to sort out its Purpose, Vision and Values. They were using multi-disciplinary action learning groups which were giving immediate, if not always comfortable, feedback on the progress on key issues and projects. The participants came up with their own classification of the staff's responses to change on what they determined were the two critical dimensions – Understanding and Energy (see Fig. 8, opposite).

They were keen that progress was made to ensure they all still had jobs. To do this they had to make sure that the number of people with little understanding or energy – 'the dinosaurs' (the people whose tails were being eaten but the message had not yet reached their brains) – was falling rapidly. But as the action learning groups set off they found that even if most of the dinosaurs started to move all was not necessarily well. There were two other groups who were much trickier to handle. One was a small group of people who had a little understanding and bags of enthusiasm. They were rushing around the organization trying to force changes along their only partly understood lines, with little feeling for the Purpose, Vision and Values, and especially behaviours, which the board intended. They got excited about ideas and then tried to impose them on others rather than helping those others to learn for themselves. Inevitably these 'dangerous enthusiasts' were a danger to the organization and themselves because their enthusiasm was misplaced.

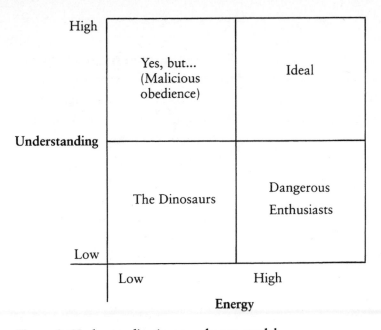

Figure 8 **Understanding/energy change model**

The other group had high understanding but little energy to change and formed the bulk of the population. They were quite capable of envisioning what was being asked of them, saw its advantages and disadvantages, and then decided that the latter were too prominent so they would not commit themselves to the changes. They were either sceptical or cynical. They created another type of organizational blockage: being unwilling to change themselves they were bright enough to see and play on the hidden problems in the proposed changes of structure and procedure. Rather than oppose directly, they would do precisely what they were asked, no more and no less, knowing that without the use of some of their own discretion things would go wrong. They used 'malicious obedience' to scupper the changes. Their 'Yes, but . . .' really meant 'no' but sounded better. They always had lots of reasons why things should not happen. If forced to take action then they would do it, grudgingly, to the letter.

The task for the board and the action learning teams was to steer the changes through the opposing rocks of dangerous enthusiasm and malicious obedience towards the ideal state. No-one had reached such a state of perfection, but by becoming aware of the problems, and by making them public – a clever poster campaign by the staff, using the four classifications, identified these blockages to change – it was possible to change considerably the emotional temperature over a six-month period. And that is fast.

Levels of Culture

Culture has three distinct levels in any organization:

Work Group
Corporate
National

Each level of culture has its own characteristics and is to an extent partly sealed off from the other levels. Therein lies a major problem for boards. How do you organize a consistent corporate culture when both the work group and the national cultures seem to be pointing in different directions? Matters are made worse by the fact that there is never a single, tangible 'organization' easily visible for the members of an enterprise. All organizations are 'virtual organizations' in that they are what each of us believes them to be. People then behave to this virtual picture. In an age of delayered, demanned, decentralized, and demystified organizations this is increasingly true. So centralized control is increasingly difficult, but a clear, central Purpose, Vision and Values can lead to a constructive aligned culture if the directors show leadership and confidence. But how does one get large numbers of people attuned to a common purpose?

WORK-GROUP CULTURE

For a board the work groups are often the most difficult cultures to penetrate and influence. Geertz's 'system of inherited conceptions' gives each work group a distinctive flavour and history despite the fact that they all work for the same enterprise. They have their own unique induction and inclusion rituals. It is obvious who is 'in' and who is 'out', regardless of technical excellence. It is clear who socializes together and who is never asked; who is the real worker, or social, leader of the group regardless of job title; and who shapes the thinking and subsequent behaviours of the group and so defines its Values – what is right or wrong, good or bad for the group.

We cannot afford to employ squads of anthropologists to monitor work groups and report to the board. But we can get directors and line managers to be more constructive listeners and observers so that they can learn how to shift large numbers of small groups towards a common goal. As one wise old chairman said to me, 'God gave me two eyes, two ears, and one mouth – and I'm sure that is the ratio he meant me to use them in.'

When British Airways conducted its successful 'Putting the Customer First' change programmes nearly a decade ago, the board and their consultants agreed that shifting attitudes and behaviours in a previously nationalized industry would be a huge task. Some of the staff had thought that even *offering* first-class seats to customers was against the notion of nationalization, and that to offer all customers high levels of service was just perverse. Working to the lowest common denominator seemed a powerful mindset at that time.

BA set about benchmarking carefully the beliefs and values of the work groups. Their findings were fascinating, if a little depressing. Despite the merger, over twenty years before, of British Overseas Airways Corporation (BOAC) and British European Airways (BEA), there were significant numbers of staff who still saw themselves as ultimately BEA or BOAC, or, due to a later merger, as

British Caledonian Airways. Some even expressed allegiance to the Polish Air Force which had been based at RAF Northholt, near Heathrow, during World War Two. Such work-group allegiances had been passed on to younger generations. Similar situations can be found just as easily in the UK, Europe, US or Asia as enterprises change, merge or are taken over. The General Electric Company has people who still talk of allegiance to English Electric or AEI, or British Thomson Houston, or the GEC, or Plessey or Ferranti, despite these mergers having become part of the corporate history. In many parts of the world staff will refer to the good old days Under Mr X or Madame Y when 'things were much better and you were properly protected and respected unlike the situation under these new owners'.

It is very human to seek out the roots of a work group's culture and to gain one's daily recognition from it. Whilst this is difficult for a team leader to control, there are plenty of techniques available to measure attitudes, values, and staff satisfaction so as to get a fix on the variations between different work groups and different levels of the corporation.

I encourage healthy organizations to crosscheck the measures of staff *and* customer satisfaction on a regular basis and treat the results very seriously in the boardroom. The patterns identified can be of immense help both in improving the customer's perception of effectiveness – to everyone's long-term advantage – and in getting staff enthused by feeding the results of the data back to them. An emphasis on such trendlines rather than just the raw data can energize a work group, whether they are under- or overperforming. 'Town meeting' sessions with the senior managers and directors to debate the meaning of the trends, and the authorizing of small action learning groups on identified key issues to both analyse and implement appropriate solutions, can have a very positive effect in getting work groups to align and attune.

This is not to suggest that work-group cultures are inherently 'wrong'. The downside to be avoided by line managers is that it can lead to overcomfortable shared assumptions and 'groupthink' over time. The upside is that the work groups give a diversity of thought and energy to an enterprise. A key law of ecology is Ross Ashby's 'Law of Requisite Variety'[11] – for any system to survive it needs sufficient difference within it to cope with environmental change. We need to value those differences – we 'clone' our work groups at the peril of the whole organization's survival.

The issue, then, is to get these diverse groups pointing in roughly the same direction and subscribing to roughly the same organizational culture. It is a classic dilemma and, ultimately, unresolvable in the short term. It usually takes years.

CORPORATE CULTURE

The majority of boards who think about 'culture' tend to see it as a single, overarching and immutable entity – the corporate culture. This is hardly surprising as most of the literature and rhetoric in the area is written as such. But it is patently not so. Even in massive multinationals bestriding the globe and having more annual turnover than ten countries' combined Gross Domestic Product, it is impossible to say that there is only one corporate culture. It is tempting, but very unwise, for boards to speak and behave as if this were so. IBM tried for years with its 'Big Blue' culture, but people from the same technical background, education system, and social background doing the same type of job did things differently. This was particularly true if they were from different nationalities. Most multinationals I know try hard to homogenize their corporate culture and get trapped in the same board dilemma as the work groups – they need uniformity to hold the organization together, but also need sufficient diversity to stop it from dying. How do we keep the dynamic balance and resolve the dilemma?

The good news is that corporate culture is also measurable, and there are many pieces of software available to allow you to do this. One I use is the questionnaire by Roger Harrison and Charles

Handy from Handy's excellent book *The Gods of Management*.[12]
It allows the director, and others, to measure their perception of
the organization's culture on four dimensions:

1. Power culture

The relationship between an all-powerful central figure, or small
group, and the people in the divisions, business units, or work
groups. The relationship is usually highly personalized and binary.
You are either doing well or you are out. The power is bestowed
in showers of gold or thunderbolts which vaporize the transgressor.
The biggest 'sin' here is for individuals or groups on the periphery
to gang up against the centre. Terrible retribution from the centre
follows inevitably.

2. Role culture

Symbolized as the front of a Grecian temple with order, calm,
rationality and systems allowing everyone to know their place, what
they can do and what they *cannot* do. It is about procedure and
precision. Since I spend a lot of my time on fourteen-hour non-stop
flights with Cathay Pacific Airways I am reassured that their engineering division is a Role culture and not a Power one. I like to think
that the bolts are done up to the correct torque.

3. Task culture

This is the craftsmanship, technical excellence, and project-based
culture. It demands delivery to quality, time and budget. There is
a deliberate tension built into it – between getting the job done
well, and developing the people who do the job so that they can
learn to increase their effectiveness and efficiency. At present it is
fashionable to strive for a Task culture whether you need one or
not. It is not easy to install, and if the board's words and actions
are out of synch over their desire for a more Task-based culture,
then it is almost impossible to create.

4. People culture

This has lots of powerful individuals doing their work professionally without a lot of external management. It is found, for example,
with barristers, TV directors and producers, hospital consultants,
boards of directors, architects and software designers. It looks great
from the outside, but just try and join it. Induction and inclusion
are tough to the point of outright exclusion. These folk usually live
in a carefully protected sealed bubble at the top, or centre, of the
organization and protect their rights fiercely.

For a board the question is which corporate culture, or range of
cultures, is appropriate for their needs. A single, dominant culture
need not be imposed on all parts of the enterprise – provided that
the Purpose, Vision and Values are clear to all and committed to.
Different parts can adopt different cultures to reach the common
end. It is a case of horses for courses.

Continuing with the airline example, it would be reasonable that
engineering is essentially a Role culture, and so should administration, accounting and the administrative parts of personnel be.
The customer-facing divisions should be essentially Task cultures,
getting passengers and planes to their destinations on time, to quality and budget. The board, marketing, people development and
finance functions should be People cultures. When crises hit there
is likely to be an ultimate Power culture based on the dominant
personality, or personalities, who will take the toughest decisions.
Hopefully this will be the board.

The board can and should benchmark corporate culture, decide
with the staff which culture is appropriate, and then train hard
towards it.

NATIONAL CULTURE

Given that the World Trade Organization is likely to be of increasing importance, and that global economic growth in the twenty-first

century is likely to be in the East and South rather than the West, it is crucial for boards to recognize and learn to work with the international dimensions of their customers and staff.

Some countries have become very good at it, despite national stereotypes which would suggest otherwise. Hong Kong, Singapore, Switzerland, the United Kingdom and New Zealand have all realized that their populations cannot sustain or increase their standards of living without continuing exports, and the encouragement of inward and outward investment.

Unfortunately, others are locked into an imperialistic mindset and expect simply to impose their corporate and national cultures on the foreigners.

I made some unexpected money in the late 1970s rescuing a number of US multinationals who had established their Europe, Middle East and Africa (EMEA) headquarters in Paris. This mindset of blending three very different areas of the world in itself betrayed a very 'American' view of geography. Paris was usually the choice of the company president, or sometimes their partner, as a pleasant place to visit with a not so different culture from the US. Then they struck great problems. The operations managers were horrified to find that the French staff acted in a quite bureaucratic and inflexible way. They did precisely what they were paid for and did it well, but would not work late or work outside their job description. They would not do others' work and turned quickly to their unions and litigation if the US managers gave orders outside their contract of employment. Data on comparative national attitudes and behaviours in organizations had been available for some twenty-five years and would have shown that it would have been culturally easier to set up in the Netherlands, the UK or Ireland, rather than the other European Union countries. The easy thinking back in the US had been, 'Well, they are Europeans like us, and Paris is a great city, so let's start on home territory and go foreign from there.' How wrong can you be?

Measuring national differences is a controversial but highly useful area. Having knowledge of the major national cultural dimensions on which your customers, strategic alliance partners, international suppliers, financiers and staff work makes for a more effective and efficient organization. Any individual with whom you work may be well outside the median, but at least by studying the cross-cultural maps you have some coordinates to guide you and help you understand how to work with the differences.

Some countries do this easily because they can tolerate high levels of uncertainty and ambiguity and make them work for them. The UK, Ireland, Sweden, Denmark, Hong Kong, Singapore, India, Malaysia, Indonesia and the Philippines are good examples. Some, like the Germanics and Latins, find it hard and work actively against such ambiguity and uncertainty. Others, namely the Japanese, work consciously and systematically to surmount their need for certainty by using third-country nationals capable of coping with the ambiguity of working between the Japanese and the workforce of the country in which they have chosen to operate. These people can be found around the world acting as a thin film of senior management lubrication between the overseas owners and the local workforce.

The two main sources of research work in this area are *Riding the Waves of Culture* by Fons Trompenaars[13] and Geert Hofstede's *Culture's Consequences*[14] and *Cultures and Organizations: The Software of the Mind*.[15]

Trompenaars focuses mainly on managers. He takes the main dimensions of national cultural difference and turns them into *dilemmas* – the sort of tricky problems which any board has to face at a strategic level and any manager at operational level (see Fig. 9).

I have found the Hofstede cross-cultural maps an excellent way of opening up the debate of likely blocks to cross-national cooperation in a neutral and educative way. From his early work with IBM in the 1970s which produced the seminal book *Culture's Consequences*, through the formation of the Institute for Research on Inter-cultural Co-operation, to the recent publication of *Cultures*

Reconciling individualism and collectivism

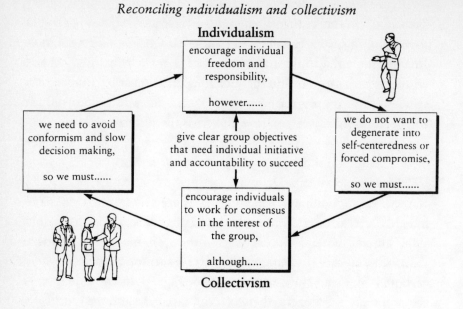

Figure 9 An example of a Trompenaars cultural dilemma

and Organizations, he has tested rigorously four initial dimensions which he thinks define national cultures:

1. Uncertainty Avoidance

The need in a *nation* for certainty, or at the other end of the scale, the ability to tolerate uncertainty and enjoy using ambiguity to achieve their ends.

2. Power Distance

The distance from national sources of power – government, army, police, taxation authorities – at which the population feels comfortable. At the authoritarian end of the scale are the dictatorships from which people want large power distances. At the other end are Western-style democracies where people want to be close to, and have a say over, the sources of power in their society.

3. Individualism/Collectivism

This is an anthropological notion of how the importance of the individual or group is valued in the national society. Australia, the US and the UK top the list of individualist societies. Most Asian, South American and African societies prefer an extended family view where the individual and the idea of 'self' is not so all-important. These are societies in which shame, rather than guilt, often determines what a person will do.

4. Masculine/Feminine

The way that a child, regardless of sex, is brought up with essentially masculine or feminine values. Britain and Sweden are remarkably close on Uncertainty Avoidance, Power Distance, and Individualism/Collectivism but are poles apart on Masculine/Feminine. Britain is, in Hofstede's terms, a 'masculine' society (essentially achievement orientated) and Sweden a 'feminine' one (essentially nurturing orientated). He was attacked for this classification in the 1970s and 1980s but in the more international 1990s people seem more willing at least to debate the findings.

These are *national* characteristics based on the median points of large samples, so there will be individual nationals who fall way outside the median. Two dimensions – Uncertainty Avoidance and Power Distance – have been found to have a close correlation to the way people think and act within their *organizations* as well as within their nation.

Hofstede's four major organizational types – village market, family, pyramid of people and well-oiled machine – will be interpreted through the emotional climate, structure, values, and behaviours in the organization. Identifying the *differences* between the national cultures allows us to understand better the dimensions on which we can become more effective in cooperating across national boundaries.

What interests me is that from the board viewpoint it is both possible and necessary to design organizations appropriately for

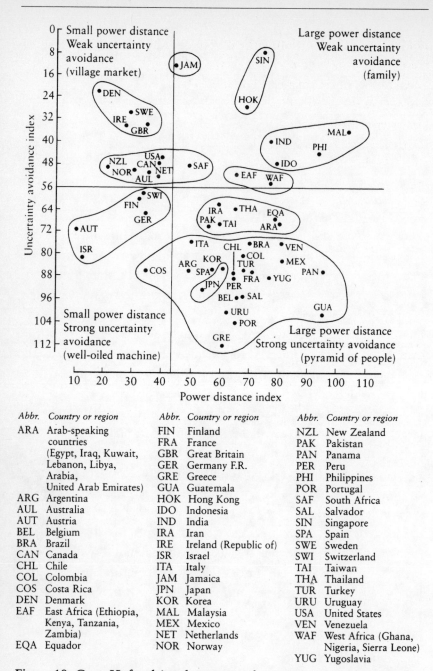

Figure 10 Geert Hofstede's culture map of uncertainty avoidance and power distance

Abbr.	Country or region	Abbr.	Country or region	Abbr.	Country or region
ARA	Arab-speaking countries (Egypt, Iraq, Kuwait, Lebanon, Libya, Arabia, United Arab Emirates)	FIN	Finland	NZL	New Zealand
		FRA	France	PAK	Pakistan
		GBR	Great Britain	PAN	Panama
		GER	Germany F.R.	PER	Peru
		GRE	Greece	PHI	Philippines
		GUA	Guatemala	POR	Portugal
ARG	Argentina	HOK	Hong Kong	SAF	South Africa
AUL	Australia	IDO	Indonesia	SAL	Salvador
AUT	Austria	IND	India	SIN	Singapore
BEL	Belgium	IRA	Iran	SPA	Spain
BRA	Brazil	IRE	Ireland (Republic of)	SWE	Sweden
CAN	Canada	ISR	Israel	SWI	Switzerland
CHL	Chile	ITA	Italy	TAI	Taiwan
COL	Colombia	JAM	Jamaica	THA	Thailand
COS	Costa Rica	JPN	Japan	TUR	Turkey
DEN	Denmark	KOR	Korea	URU	Uruguay
EAF	East Africa (Ethiopia, Kenya, Tanzania, Zambia)	MAL	Malaysia	USA	United States
		MEX	Mexico	VEN	Venezuela
		NET	Netherlands	WAF	West Africa (Ghana, Nigeria, Sierra Leone)
EQA	Equador	NOR	Norway	YUG	Yugoslavia

intercultural cooperation. For example, on the Power Distance axis many nations on the left of the map will want shallow hierarchies and a means of commenting on what is happening nationally. Those nations on the right will want organizations with a clear hierarchy, clear rights for the people with power, and some duties of protection for their staff. As a very crude rule of thumb I would say that those countries in the top two quadrants have a good chance of working together provided the individuals concerned do not come from extremes of the population. The bottom two quadrants will have more difficulty working with the others, but if they acknowledge this and can tolerate at least some of the differences then they will be able to work across national boundaries.

As interest in world trade expands we have to find ways for such cooperation. It is important that the board is sensitive to, and works on, the process of learning to work across international boundaries rather than leaving it to chance and the Brownian Motion of managers wandering the international trade paths.

With this in mind, Sir Colin Marshall of the highly international British Airways has announced a *Code of Business Conduct* which seeks to give an ethical base to their relations with customers, business partners, competitors and suppliers. Even in freewheeling Hong Kong the Communist-owned CITIC Pacific has issued an *Ethical Code of Conduct* backed by the Independent Commission Against Corruption, and some three hundred listed companies have drawn up their own codes. NatWest's code contains relevant and straightforward advice, for example, 'We believe in fair and open competition and, therefore, obtaining information about competitors by deception is unacceptable . . . making disparaging comments about competitors invariably invites disrespect from customers and should be avoided . . . Employment with NatWest must never be used in an attempt to influence public officials or customers for personal gain or benefit', and involves a system by which the code can be audited and monitored.[16] As they become more international these companies realize that there is a need to change the 'rules of engagement' with customers, staff and suppliers both to take into account the differences of others, and to ensure against corruption.

For a massive directoral challenge, try linking together the fifteen national cultures of the European Union on the Hofstede map. You can see that regardless of the political and economic dimensions this is the world's biggest cross-cultural experiment in attempting to link together three of the four major national, and organizational, cultures. Despite anything that the Maastricht Conference said, or the Inter-Governmental Conference declares, it will take at least half a century to get any significant attitudinal and behavioural shifts – and even then these may not be towards homogeneity. The cultural differences may well overcome the rhetoric of political and economic union.

These three socio-emotional elements of Policy – Purpose, Vision and Values and Culture – create the energy with which to drive the enterprise forward. They create 'the heart of the firm'. They need to be balanced, by the board, with a more hard-edged systems-structural element: the way we draw in information from the outside world.

MONITORING THE EXTERNAL ENVIRONMENT

A lot has been written on the need for the board to monitor external events. It is an integral aspect of all of the four Directoral Dilemmas. My experience is that most boards' thinking portfolios are hardly in touch with the present world, prefer the past, and find the future a very threatening land. Because most have come from a managerial and professional background, their thinking processes have evolved naturally over time away from scanning for the 'hard facts' (what can be measured easily) towards intuiting from the 'soft facts' (what can be sensed). They rely on their ability to *sense* what is happening and relate that to their successful past actions. This has a negative effect both in that they fail to monitor the external environment and that they supervise management only from the board's retrospective perspective.

Most of the boards and directors I meet do not have systematic routines for scanning the changing external environment and are, consequently, frequently wrong-footed by sudden changes over which they have no control and which they do not fully understand. It is a classic dilemma. Their initial response has to be a quick damage-limitation and assessment exercise. Then the more daunting task is to *think* about what the changes mean. Learning Boards go much further than damage limitation. They think about and then actively design their future.

Here I want to focus on the process of bringing managers and professionals away from their inward-looking, organizational efficiency-orientated behaviours towards budgeting some of their directoral time to learn how to think and reflect on policy and strategy issues – by following and comparing trends in the external environment.

The first step is for directors not to feel guilty if they are found reading a daily paper or professional journal at their desk. They need to stop behaving as if the only 'real' work is in taking action.

How do you get people to budget even five percent of their time for looking outwards?

A board can start scanning the environment simply by setting up the personal and group rigour of reading daily and weekly newspapers, and then learning the skill of taking an item and asking 'What does this mean for us?' *The Economist* or *Newsweek* or *Asia Business* or *The Far East Economic Review*, for example, all help give concise pictures of the week past and the possible times ahead and can help set an intellectual structure within which a board can think. Making time for discussion with other board or management members, ensuring that there is space in board meetings or at coffee, or lunch, or drinks for such regular discussions and then logging or benchmarking them for further observation would put your board in the upper quartile of the boards I have encountered. Learning to connect any news item – local, regional, national, international, trade, science, arts, sport, as well as business – is a key directoral skill. It means a board doesn't have to rubber stamp decisions which were made elsewhere and brought to them as a formality because they have the time and capacity to think for themselves.

It can be quite a revelation for a new board member to discover just how much time can be created once he or she stops intervening back into the managerial world at the first hint of a crisis. There is no lack of ways in which to use this extra time.

Scanning is *not* about ensuring precise and accurate predictions about the future. Taking any of the think-tank reports about the future from, say, ten years ago shows just how wrong they can be – but they may have had the germ of a useful idea there. The board's task is to be *sensitized* to future possibilities, not predict them. They need to spot the 'weak signals' that may identify future significant change, to use a chaos theory analogy. Such changes may, or may not, happen. But being sensitive to the possibility of such events allows greater confidence and less need to panic as the future unfolds. It also means that the board can take a constructive approach to designing their own organization's future.

'Hearing the baby cry' is an analogy boards with whom I have worked have found useful.[17] Parents are so sensitized to their own child that despite all sorts of loud background noise they are capable of hearing *their* baby cry. How sensitive is your board to hearing your baby cry? For some action-orientated, binary and convergent thinking boards such analyses are anathema. Fine. But they are then doomed to stay stuck in their managerial world and will not make effective *direction-givers*.

Once the basic discipline of scanning the environment regularly and rigorously, making coherent patterns and debating them is installed on a board, then more sophisticated techniques can be pursued. There is a growing number of on-line information services which can provide incredible amounts of data – from the World Wide Web to company-specific information. One can go further still and set up Competitor Intelligence processes which regularly monitor the products and behaviours of the competition. This does not mean large sums of money being spent on industrial spying, although one national airline is reported to have set up monitoring devices in their first-class airline seats for that purpose. It means scanning publicly available material – professional journals, press interviews and conference papers, for example, with some sensitivity and then tracing the changing patterns of their investment and technologies in relation to your own.

When I was in China towards the end of the Cultural Revolution it was noticeable that young Japanese students were beginning to appear in the student dormitories of the major universities. On enquiring it turned out that their employers, the major Japanese corporations, were 'seeding' the universities, and Chinese society, with a generation of Japanese who would grow up with, and dedicate their lives to, working with their Chinese student colleagues. The Japanese corporate thinking was that when eventually their Chinese colleagues came to power they would be inextricably linked with them, socially and professionally.

Such long-term policy thinking is typical of the Asian approach to investment in people, as well as industries. It helps resolve some of the many uncertainties about the future without trying to predict with accuracy the likely out-turns. Their approach is a lesson in playing 'the infinite game', and learning from doing so, rather than playing the 'finite game' (win or lose) by which most Westerners are fixated.

At the extreme end of the environmental scanning, or future-watching, industry there are think-tanks and pressure groups which are playing an increasingly powerful role in Western societies. Boards must learn how to cope with, and use, their outputs without compromising their own policies.

Shell UK found this out to their cost in the summer of 1995 over the Brent Spar rig decommissioning incident (see page 177).

More and more enterprises are investing in future-watching processes. Microsoft has created the Advanced Technology Group, Toshiba now has a Lifestyles Research Institute, and Yamaha has imaginatively established a 'listening post' in London which it acknowledges as the world's music capital. It has filled the post with the latest musical electronic technologies which is then made available to the best of Europe's musical talent, whilst Yamaha watches and logs what they do, and what they demand for the future.

Once scanning systems are established, a board can begin to address the impact of external changes on policy, and *how* these policies will be implemented – in other words, strategy. The board's capacity for strategic thinking is what we now turn to.

CHAPTER 4

Strategic Thinking

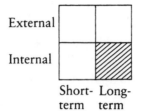

Organizational effectiveness: Long-term, internally-oriented thinking

Strategy is about the *delivery* of the enterprise's Purpose. To achieve this most businesses require at least three distinct strategies – Business, Financial and People Development.

I am against the notion of strategic *planning* at board level because it means getting bogged down in planning and numbers which takes the board's minds away from strategic *thinking*. I am with Henry Mintzberg, who says that strategic planning is an oxymoron, like 'friendly fire', 'fun run' or 'military intelligence'.[18] Although planning is vital to the health of any organization, it should happen immediately *below* the level of the Learning Board model. Strategic *thinking* is the director's role.

But it is not only the directors who need to fuel the strategic thinking. People both within and without the organization will have valuable inputs to make and should be consulted, even if the ultimate responsibility and liability for strategy lies firmly with the board and the directors.

The Brain of the Board

I see the board as the central processor of the business brain. They are at the centre of a series of overlapping circles of influence and ideas. Staff, customers, stakeholders and politicians/legislators are all monitoring and creating change and so provide the coordinates within which strategic thinking can take place. Feedback to the board from customers, competitor intelligence systems, the enactment of legislation nationally and internationally, local and wider community issues, international economic, political and trade trends helps the board's developing sense of the changing environments. There are many techniques available for ensuring this happens: action learning groups, town meetings, mass debates, teleconferencing, e-mail, or the InterNet all have their place.

A healthy business brain comes from two sources:

1. A capacity on the board to use and value a portfolio of thinking styles and processes when debating and problem-solving.
2. A capacity to think in such a way that the outcome is implementable. A half-good strategy well implemented is worth more to an organization than a brilliant strategy which is not implementable.

Henry Mintzberg has produced a drawing (see opposite) which demonstrates his idea of 'strategy as seeing'.[19]

This is helpful because it shows that we are not just talking about thinking but about the range of visual perceptions we create from our thinking – seeing ahead, seeing behind, seeing above, seeing below, seeing beyond, seeing beside and, finally, seeing through. Contained within this is the key psychological notion of the ability to 'reframe' what is being seen. It is its ability to make better, more comprehensive, more imaginative pictures about the past, present and future which helps differentiate a board from its competitors.

Most managers and professionals, as distinct from artists and poets, are taught to think 'convergently'. They focus on an issue

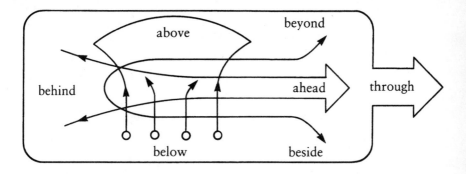

Figure 11 Henry Mintzberg's 'strategic thinking as seeing' model

quickly, then discard any possibilities and environmental signals they evaluate as 'irrelevant', before focusing on a single 'right' solution. In this way they generate high certainty, but also a high risk of being wrong. This is good for managers but bad for direction-givers. If directors think like this then they will be tempted ultimately to put all their eggs in one basket and bet the company on a single strategy.

Strategic, or 'divergent', thinking tends to a 'both . . . and' style of thought. A single answer is not accepted as good enough. We need to generate imagination, creativity, and ingenuity in order to create a much higher quality *range* of answers, where two apparently incompatible answers are simultaneously possible. Binary thinkers find this almost inconceivable – but who said organizational life was simple or easy?

I have put together a ten-step process of strategic thinking which has helped many boards. It is not a miracle cure, but it does help expand the portfolio of strategic thinking skills within the board, and leads to better quality reframing of what is 'seen'. It means developing systematically a capacity to adopt a 'helicopter view'. Starting at ground level, we climb to a height where the board is stretched but still comfortable. After that we have the option to go stratospheric . . .

THE TEN-STEP STRATEGIC-THINKING PROCESS
Three Basic Steps

1. SWOTS AND PPESTT

At ground level one needs to start at, and return regularly to, a bench-mark. This is the function of the SWOT analysis (see Fig. 12). SWOTs – Strengths, Weaknesses, Opportunities and Threats – are the corner-stone of the board's strategic thinking, especially of its debates. The board needs a firm grip on both the internal aspects of the SWOT – the Strengths and Weaknesses of the enterprise – and the external – Opportunities and Threats. Whatever other strategic thinking tech-niques they use, the board must create a discipline to return regularly and rigorously to define their SWOTs. It is a crucial part of the annual cycle of a board. Without this they will drift directionless. If this hap-pens then the corporate head has started to rot.

The Organizational Climate Survey is a useful tool on the intern-ally-orientated Strengths and Weaknesses side. This *must* be under-taken with known competitors firmly in mind. The PPESTT analysis – of Political, Physical, Economic, Social, Technological and Trade environments – is an equally useful thinking tool on the externally-orientated Opportunities and Threats side.

However sophisticated our strategic thinking becomes, it is to the SWOT that we need always to return to check and then reframe our strategic thinking.

2. THE VALUE CHAIN

To get a board's 'thinking helicopter' a few hundred feet off the ground, so that they can begin to experiment with perspective and angle, to see things in a different light, it is important for all board members to understand the ways in which value is added to the

To be protected and developed	STRENGTHS	OPPORTUNITIES
To be avoided or changed	WEAKNESSES	THREATS
	Internal Orientation	External Orientation

Figure 12 The SWOT analysis

enterprise, public or private. There are a number of instruments for doing this. I have found Michael Porter's Value Chain model[20] of particular help here in reframing the board's thinking:

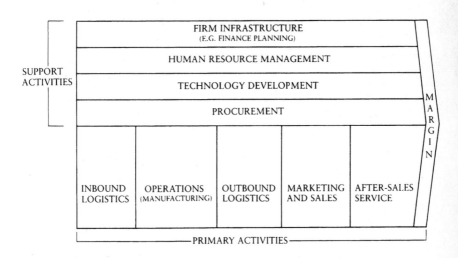

Figure 13 The Value Chain

Working through each of the Value Chain's Primary Activities and Support Activities must, crucially, be done in relation to *known* competitors. It is important that the board is ruthlessly honest with itself over the inputs and the results, even if it turns up inevitable gaps in its competitor intelligence system, and if the results show that they are no different from anyone else. This is vital information. If customers cannot distinguish between your business and any other they will simply buy on price. You have then been 'commoditized' – the biggest corporate sin of all. It is one of the the board's primary tasks to so differentiate the product or service that it has an added value to the customer. If successful then you can charge a small premium on price and keep ahead of the price wars of the commoditized competitors.

A pharmaceutical client of mine, a world leader, went through such a value chain process. To the outside world they are a model of research-driven and marketing excellence. That is their carefully nurtured public profile. It is true that they spend huge sums of money in both areas. But so do their competitors.

In a ruthless review of where value was really added in relation to their known competitors they found that a main distinguishing function was in an unfashionable, low-profile, back-office area. They had seen that in the future new chemical entity development would depend crucially on being able to reduce the industry's very long 'time to market' – the length of time from the initial idea for the new product to having the drug patented, accredited, and in the pharmacy. This often took twelve years by the end of all testing. With a patent lasting, until recently, for just fifteen years, this meant that the chances of having an even semi-monopolistic market for any length of time were low. They set about a rigorous codification programme of all the necessary certification and acceptance procedures needed by the authorities in each of their major markets around the world, knowing that the whole would be driven by the demands of the Food and Drug Administration in the US. By developing a core competence in this seemingly prosaic area they added value dramatically by reducing time to market through streamlining all the national procedures. Whereas their major competitors can deliver a new drug onto roughly three markets simultaneously they can do it in more than thirty. This has very positive effects on their profitability.

3. THE FIVE FORCES MODEL

Rising higher in the helicopter, and achieving even broader perspectives, a board can increase further their understanding of their competitive position and the changing environments in which they create their ecological energy niches. Again there are a number of tools available, but I have been influenced strongly in my thinking by another Michael Porter idea – the Five Forces model (see below).[21] Here the board investigates rigorously, with the help of many of its people, including its many 'stakeholders', the major forces creating that changing environment:

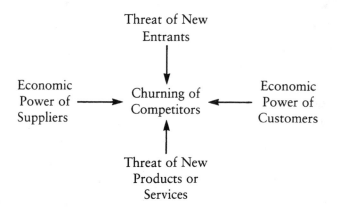

Figure 14 Michael Porter's Five Forces model

Once again, it is crucial that this is undertaken systematically and dispassionately, and that there is careful comparison with known competitors. The competitor analysis system and the processes for monitoring the external environment are valuable here.

On the vertical axis it is important to assess the cost of entry for new competitors, or new products or services, as well as the probability of this happening. In industries like pharmaceuticals the financial cost of entry, in terms of setting up large manufacturing, distribution and marketing systems, is high. In other industries, like my own multi-media one, a single talented person working from home with a powerful personal computer and a few contacts can offer very low-cost services.

On the horizontal axis the power of suppliers – of people, services, hardware or raw materials – can be high. Recent experiences with computer chip manufacturers and paper suppliers are good examples of monopoly suppliers naming their own prices. On the power of customers side, some have developed such great strength that they have finally had to back off for fear of strangling their industry. They have tended to specify so tightly in, say, food or clothing or electronic component supply from the input of materials to the final position on the retailers' shelves that they have effectively ended up running their suppliers' as well as their own businesses. They become the dominant or even monopoly customer. This is economically unwise for both parties. Even when they have backed off so that, for example, they will take only sixty percent of a single supplier's total output, they can still overspecify in such areas as distribution and logistics. It is common, for instance, for supermarkets to give a supplier a fifteen minute slot to get their truck into the loading bay or lose the ability to deliver for that day or week, with the consequent loss to the supplier. They auction key positions on their supermarket shelves and have all sorts of other tactics for trying to increase their low margins. Life is tough when you are commoditized.

If you set up systems which regularly and rigorously monitor and debate environmental changes and have ways of turning them into implementable plans, then you are already doing better than seventy-five percent of the boards I see around the world, both big organizations and small. Regularly updating, say at six-monthly intervals, your SWOT in line with the first three steps of strategic thinking is a powerful development process for your portfolio of strategic thinking skills. It also helps create the annual rhythm of the board's work. However, it is wise to budget board time to learn how to go further still.

Advanced Steps

4. ENVIRONMENTAL VARIABLES

Regular use of the SWOT analysis begins to give the board a clear feel of the patterns in those areas which are of key importance to their enterprise. Which are the variables on which you must always focus to out-think the competition? Do not just accept the industry norms for these. Use your divergent thinking capacities to generate a wide range of possibilities before beginning to evaluate them. Most directors evaluate possibilities much too early on, narrowing their sights and losing most of their opportunities.

A list of these key variables for a US retail bank is:

Interest rates
Savings ratios
Demographic trends
Lifestyle trends
US trade trends
Government spending

Scenarios and Dilemmas
From here the board begins to go stratospheric in its quality of strategic thinking to drive the business forward. If you budget board time here then you are on the way to joining the top ten percent.

It takes some investment of board time to learn how to handle scenarios effectively. A skill developed at Shell International, Motorola and British Airways, amongst others, it requires serious use of the board's intellect. However, at this point many director/

managers plead airsickness and want to return to operations. If, after selection and training, they still feel the same, then let them go back. At this level we are looking for people committed to direction-giving and capable of riding the winds of uncertainty.

We are trying to use at least three of the Chinese philosopher and strategist Sun Tzu's thoughts on strategy[22] to achieve these higher states of strategic thinking:

1. The supreme act of warfare is to subdue the enemy without fighting . . . use strategy to bend others without coming into conflict.
2. He who can look into the future and discern conditions that are not yet manifest will invariably win.
3. He who only sees the obvious wins battles with difficulty; he who looks below the surface of things wins with ease.

With scenarios we are looking for possible *combinations* of future events against which to test our thinking. It is highly unlikely that the future will throw up any of the precise combinations debated. That is not important. The principle here is that directors learn from working on these combinations, revisiting and changing them regularly. A simplistic set of 'best case and worst case' scenarios are little use because they take us straight back to binary and convergent thinking, and a focus on prediction. We are trying to escape the need for such certainties, to give the board and senior managers a sufficiently wide perspective and sufficiently flexible thinking that *whatever* happens they are likely to have thought through and discussed it in relation to their Purpose, Vision and Values, and strategic intent, and to have debated appropriate contingency actions.

It is a paradox that when thinking strategically we need to be uncertain if we are to give useful direction. A company needs to be sensitized to the changing environment and capable of ditching a strategy without straying from its Purpose. I know major companies who will abandon a carefully developed strategy weeks after announcing it to the press and analysts – if there has been significant environmental change. They may feel a little foolish but this is preferable to betting the company on a known loser.

As an example, the British Airways Customer Relations team was reported to have been taking time out off-line to develop scenarios.[23] Two of the number they developed were:

Wild gardens

A world in which market forces are unleashed in the airline world. Asian markets grow rapidly. The US, after a period of low growth, falls into a deep recession at the start of the next century. In the UK the Conservatives win the 1996 election but remain divided over Europe. The European Union is enlarged eastwards but there is no agreement on the single currency. The European Union, however, takes over negotiating airline agreements for member governments. It reaches an Atlantic Open Skies agreement which gives the EU and North American airlines free access to transatlantic routes and some access to US and EU domestic airports.

New structures

This is a non-stable scenario giving governments greater control and allowing a slower rise in Asia. A Labour government is elected in the UK which joins France and Germany in promoting European integration. The EU agrees a single currency, the Euromarque, and promotes integrated air traffic control and a high-speed rail network. There is increased commitment to the environment. In the US President Clinton and the Republican Congress agree to work together to promote investment and increase productivity. Taxes are increased and defence expenditure cut. There is a security crisis in Asia involving North Korea. China suffers after the death of Deng Xiaoping. Investment in Asia is reduced.

These scenarios helped develop a range of thoughts about possibilities and threats, what the scenarios might mean to their enterprise, and what, if anything, they could do about it. Expansion in Asia, as shown in 'Wild Gardens', was thought by the customer service team to suggest, amongst other things, that they would have to forget about English being the international language as they would have more customers speaking Asian languages than English. One of the issues emerging from the 'New Structures' scenario was that if it came to pass then a greater emphasis will be put on ethical issues for companies. Customers would be expected to be treated better. The customer relations folk are developing a Customer's Charter to cope with this.

5. CALCULUS

Such scenarios are then carefully analysed in depth to precipitate a calculus, a mathematical calculation using symbols, to reach the essence of each scenario – the specific directoral dilemmas for the board. This is the acid test of their 'both ... and' thinking and leads us naturally into the *dilemma* arena. A dilemma has two irreconcilable poles, or horns – how do we do this *and* that? This is where the intellectual capacity of the board is stretched and tested. Shown opposite is an example from Charles Hampden-Turner's chapter in *Developing Strategic Thought*.[24]

There are three calculuses within the drawing: the American approach – the Triumph of Creativity – starts with the brilliant, innovating and designed strategy and works through to its total faith in the sovereignty of markets. The second calculus – Greater Europe Rebounds – starts with systematically raising standards of quality and benchmarking and finishes by forming a 'value star' co-created with customers. The third calculus – Japan Rides the Chinese Tiger – begins again by means of brilliant innovation and designed strategy and ends with taking converging paths to future rendezvous.

A *strategy cycle*

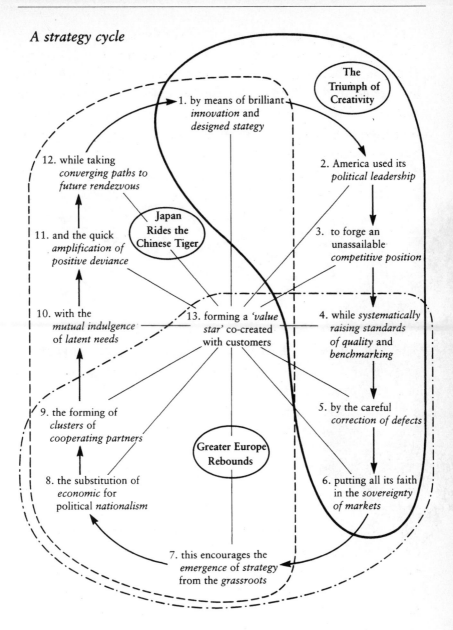

Figure 15 An example of Charles Hampden-Turner's calculus

6. STRATEGIC IMPLICATIONS

This can start either after the Five Forces model-style analysis, or, in more advanced boards, after the scenarios and dilemmas. From here the process can proceed with consideration of the strategic *implications* for the enterprise of the strategic thinking so far – through intra-board and in-company debates, discussions, and implementation plans. Some boards use formal debates, others use focus groups, some use two-way briefings, others e-mail discussions.

7. STRATEGIES TO ACHIEVE THE PURPOSE

Decisions are then taken by the board, especially on the Business, Financial, and People Development strategies, in line with the agreed policies. Remember that, despite all the rhetoric about 'strategy', the basic strategies are very simple – advance, retreat, hold your position, make alliances, or surrender. It is essential to be clear about the direction of each strategy for each business unit. This gives credible leadership and, most importantly, makes them more easily implementable by the staff.

8. STRATEGIC ALLOCATION OF RESOURCES

The board takes decisions on the strategic allocation of scarce organizational resources to ensure that the strategies are implementable. If the strategy is not able to be implemented, drop it.

9. START THE PLANNING PROCESS

Note that it is only now that planning starts in earnest. The strategic thinking is changed into an operational process by the managers in line with policies, strategies and resources decided by the board.

10. INSTALL THE FEEDBACK PROCESSES
TO THE BOARD

These must be implemented so that information about the quality of its information and decision-taking flows back to the board through its supervision of management learning cycle, thereby reinforcing the processes of the Learning Organization and the Learning Board.

The Ten-Step Process of Strategic Thinking is a fundamental part of board training and development and is the ultimate responsibility of the chairman in agreement with the chief executive.

What we are trying to avoid here is the rush into planning at the expense of strategic thought, a global problem.

I saw an example of this with the Arabian Gulf branches of an East Asian bank. Each branch had a 'strategic planning process'. They took three days out at the start of their 'planning round'. Of this some two to three hours was spent on a rather desultory conversation about the outside world and its changes. This was over by coffee. Then the 'real' work began – fighting for budgets and projects – and the rest of the three days was spent rationalizing a wish-list into a plausible document for those above. This was sent to regional headquarters in their required format. Here it waited for around a month whilst others added and subtracted parts without much reference to the originators. The figures, with very little commentary, were then sent on to headquarters. Here the head office people amended them with little reference back, but in line with what they knew of the board's wishes. The consolidated figures were finally presented to the board where a rather stilted discussion ensued and the strategic plans for their world view was agreed. After the board meeting the chairman added some amendments of his own, especially for the Gulf since he had recently been talking on a plane with a fellow who knew what was likely to happen there. Then the results were sent from the board to regional headquarters, who amended them again and passed them finally, after nearly a three-month process, to each country branch. Nobody recognized the final figures, nobody felt emotionally committed to them, and few had any idea how to achieve what they saw as others' targets.

Sadly this is not an uncommon example of a non-learning strategic planning process.

The development of board competencies in Policy Formulation and Strategic Thinking give an undoubted edge and lead to a Performing Board. Both of these, the right-hand side of the Learning Board model, often lead to discomfort amongst directors as they fight to shake off their earlier convengent thinking styles. Perseverance in changing mindsets and learning to use uncertainty to advantage can have great benefits for a board in raising itself above competitors and 'industry formulas'.

Now we turn our focus away from Board Performance towards the two aspects of Board *Conformance* – supervision of management, and accountability – which counterbalance the forward drive of policy and strategy by ensuring prudent control, so maintaining the dynamic balance of the four Directoral Dilemmas.

CONFORMANCE ASPECTS
OF THE BOARD

CHAPTER 5

Supervision of Management

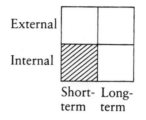

Organizational efficiency: Short-term, internally-oriented thinking

Unless the board chairman handles the Supervision of Management by the directors carefully, this is the black hole into which all the board's energies can be sucked, never to reappear. Lack of good Supervision of Management combined with weak management information systems can create the scale of corporate upset that reaches the front pages of the world's newspapers.

At the time of writing, the collapse of Barings merchant bank and the activities of a rogue trader at Daiwa Bank's New York offices are international news. Both traders allegedly dramatically exceeded their levels of authority: the continuing enquiries are revealing weak managerial and financial controls in each bank. Schneider are also under scrutiny for allegations of laxness of managerial, especially financial, controls across a number of related companies, and there are similar allegations about the astonishing loss of some £800 million by the Church Commissioners of the Church of England through disastrous property speculations in the 1980s with monies notionally held in stewardship on behalf of the Anglican clergy and parishioners. In each case the financial and social losses were large.

We also see corporate governance problems in Germany with Metallgesellschaft, Volkswagen, or Mercedes Benz, in France with Suez and Disney World, and in the the US with IBM or General Motors. These are recognized by the companies and are being tackled through better controls, and rightly so. It is the board's role to install robust and regularly maintained systems.

Let's remind ourselves of what the IOD *Standards for the Board* says about the roles of the board in the area of Supervision of Management, what they call 'Delegation to Management':

'. . . keeping [the enterprise] under prudent control'

'. . . the board is required to be sufficiently knowledgeable about the workings of the company to be answerable for its actions'

'. . . the board must be sensitive to short-term, local issues'

'. . . the board is expected to be focused on the commercial needs of the business while acting responsibly towards its employees, business partners, and society as a whole'.

Observing Patterns

Standards makes some heroic assumptions about the competence of direction-givers. Such competence *can* be reached – through director training and development – but, as we know, most directors have been managers and professionals and are constantly seduced by a tempting crisis to slip back into the managerial or professional role. The trade-off is in not leading the enterprise.

I have found, using the Thinking Intentions Profile instrument (see p.195), that the vast majority of directors are not comfortable processing the 'hard' facts – accounts, budgets and so on. They can do it, but it is one of their least preferred styles of thinking and so is done only moderately well. They are much better at dealing with the 'soft' facts – sensing what is happening. The result is that most directors tend to *sense* what is occurring rather than to check on what the hard, visibly measurable facts are. To be able to supervise management effectively, a director needs both a mindset which allows him or her to take data and find patterns within it, and decent systems to provide reliable data in the first place. I have rarely seen both in my travels around the world.

My findings – not just of a lack of systems for the supervision of management, but also of an active dislike of them – have been corroborated in the UK. The Cadbury Committee on 'The Financial Aspects of Corporate Governance'[25] has caused worldwide interest and debate. One of its recommendations was that the board needs to state that financial controls of the business are reviewed and in good order. This has caused outrage amongst many of the top-500 companies. Curiously they have seemingly been encouraged by one of the biggest accountancy firms. KPMG is reported to have told its clients in May 1995 that 'while for accounting periods beginning on or after January 1 1995, the directors *are* required to confirm that they have reviewed the effectiveness of the system, they are *not* [my italics] required to state their actual opinion on effectiveness – although the guideline notes that they may wish to do so, something we advise against strongly'.[26] This must be puzzling for shareholders and other stakeholders who have assumed, reasonably, that a top-500 company would have robust financial reporting systems in place. Apparently this is not so.

Research from Ernst & Young published in July 1995 shows that 'almost 40% of top companies have no internal audit service', whilst some 66 percent of finance directors believe that the skills of their internal audit service need strengthening. 'Less than 50% of companies with an internal audit service are confident that their monitoring will be an adequate input to the directors' report on internal control under Cadbury ... There is a widely held view amongst finance directors that external auditors and line management confirmation procedures provide an adequate basis of assurance for internal control. In a similar way audit committee chairmen most commonly rely on the finance directors to provide requisite assurance'. Only 40 percent of finance directors claimed to be very confident that their internal audit department had the skills to deal with these issues.

Interestingly, some of these control issues are put down to problems with the current fashion for 'business re-engineering' – often one of the first groups to be 'downsized' is internal audit, because they are not front-line folk. Such short-termism can lead to apparent organizational efficiency at the cost of later organizational ineffectiveness, lowered customer satisfaction and poor public perception. And remember that the above figures are for the UK's top-500 businesses.

Just how effective is your Supervision of Management?

The most common comment I hear from the directors with whom I work is that they are nervous because they have no real way of knowing whether the facts and figures on which they are basing their decisions are correct. They rely on sensing what is going on, based on previous experience, but feel that this may not be valid. This is the essence of the Directoral Dilemma: you can't know everything, but ultimately you are held responsible. To achieve any sort of confidence one needs at the minimum two types of measure:

Key Performance Indicators
 and
Overseeing of Managerial Performance.

Key Performance Indicators

FINANCIAL PERFORMANCE

An essential building block of any key performance indicator system must be the financial performance of the organization. An essence of financial performance is cash flow. Despite all the financial rhetoric and buzz-words, in the final analysis 'cash is king' will always be true. It is easy to go bust on a theoretically profitable project or business just by running out of cash. It happens every day.

An example of this was a near-disaster in an Asian transnational company. For this usually cash-rich company a cash crisis was logically impossible, but in an attempt to reach his 're-engineering' target a manager had sacked over ninety percent of the invoice clerks. This had a marvellous effect on his bottom line, but within three months the whole company was in crisis because insufficient invoices had been sent to cover the cash flow. The company had to be refinanced rapidly at large expense. This involved a change in ownership power and it will never be quite the same again. The good news is that they have learned from it and have much better cash management systems in place.

Directors need to understand not only cash flow but also the profit and loss accounts and the balance sheet. All should be studied within their context. A director needs to be able to see the changing pattern of the figures and their relationship to each other. Simply reading one set of figures is not sufficient, even if you understand them. You need to see the history, and the present position, to be able to think effectively about the future. This can be difficult for the single-function manager, or professional, who has been trained only in convergent thinking. It is the point at which they may unofficially drop out of a board and revert to their functional specializations, thereby reducing the diversity of thought possible whilst increasing the likely number of crises in the operations cycle. The chairman must take a leading, and developmental, role in ensuring that the directors are competent to deal with the financial figures. He or she must have the figures presented in such a way that they show the trends and relationships as clearly as possible so that the projected consequences of the information can be the main focus of the Supervision of Management aspect of the board.

This idea of using patterning is very important for the board if they are to keep a focus on their policy and strategy objectives. The Prudential Assurance Company based in London has computer screens set into the boardroom table so that each director can access a *visual* picture of the figures which they can then manipulate through 'What if . . . ?' questioning. As such software becomes more widely available then the possibility of using interactive graphic systems, instead of just lists of numbers, should enhance greatly the quality of boardroom debates.

RATIOS AND TRENDLINES

For some twenty-five years the General Electric Company has controlled around two hundred companies through very rigorous monthly reporting on seven financial ratios and twelve trendlines (see Tables 2 and 3).

Table 2   GEC's 'Seven Ratios'

$$1. \quad \frac{\text{Profit}}{\text{Sales}}$$

$$2. \quad \frac{\text{Sales}}{\text{Capital employed}}$$

$$3. \quad \frac{\text{Profit}}{\text{Capital employed}}$$

$$4. \quad \frac{\text{Sales}}{\text{Inventories}}$$

$$5. \quad \frac{\text{Sales}}{\text{Debtors}}$$

$$6. \quad \frac{\text{Sales}}{\text{No. of employees}}$$

7.   Sales per £/$ of emoluments

Providing they are pointing in the right direction and are moving at the right speed, then all is well with the business as far as headquarters is concerned. Should they be pointing in the wrong direction then headquarters knows what the issues are, if not the details,

Table 3   GEC's 'Twelve Trendlines'

1. Sales (£/$)

2. Orders received

3. Orders in hand

4. Net profit

5. Direct wages

6. Overhead spend

7. Capital employed

8. Stock levels

9. Trade debtors

10. No. of employees
     direct
     indirect

11. Average wages per hour of direct labour
     basic rates
     including premium payments

12. Export sales (from total sales)

so will demand rapid correction until the figures are back on track. They will not intervene directly, but the reporting channels become quite hot until resolution is reached.

In themselves these are not formulae which can be applied easily everywhere: they are essentially efficiency-orientated and do not address the customer perception measures. However, the beauty of such measuring tools is that, through demonstrating the overall patterns of a business, they do set a discipline for Supervision of Management. If you then add the 'soft' measures of customer and staff satisfaction and retention, and supplier, shareholder and stakeholder feedback, you can create a strong framework within which a board can regularly and consistently view its total organizational performance.

Lists of figures and reams of computer printout lead quite understandably to eye-rolling amongst directors, but directors need to know the trends they are describing, in other words the direction in which the figures are pointing, so that these can be checked against the strategies proposed to achieve the organization's purpose.

PROJECT MANAGEMENT

As businesses decentralize and strive to create smaller, more manageable business units it is necessary for the Supervision of Management approach to become more focused on project management skills to keep the whole together.

Business development and the managed decline of units can all be project managed. Joint venture and strategic alliances also have to be project managed from the board's viewpoint. Companies like ABB are taking this idea to its current logical conclusion by moving their business units towards becoming 'federations'. Doing this means consciously managing units with inbuilt tensions created by using a matrix of both functional and country management. These units in themselves will not necessarily be of sufficient size to bid for the scale of project they have to win in the international markets. They must, therefore, be skilful at managing their *internal* contracting process to create alliances large enough to do so. Directors and managers orientated towards an 'organizational efficiency only' approach hate this as they have to budget time for negotiating the internal inputs and outputs with their colleagues towards an agreed common goal instead of living comfortably within their previous 'personal bottom line' thinking. The business performance of these early 'federal' structures looks promising and seems to be much more in line with the customer needs of the twenty-first century.

A good example of the rigorous project management approach is shown at Japan's Kao Corporation, makers of floppy disks. They pursued what is now known as 'Discovery Driven Planning'[27] to challenge consistently the *inbuilt* assumptions of their directors and managers, and developed a system which involved such novel ideas as 'reverse income statements', 'performance operations specs', 'key assumptions checklists' and the better known 'milestone planning charts'. I have shown in Figure 16 (overleaf) an example of the levels of rigour they go into when checking the 'Milestone events' against the 'Assumptions to be tested'. How many boards and managements do you know that invest time to achieve this level of intellectual rigour?

Again, I am not suggesting that directors themselves take such direct action. I am looking for the derivation of Key Performance Indicators which show positive and negative deviations from the strategies and plans which will deliver ultimately the organization's purpose.

Overseeing of Managerial Performance

Creating the Key Performance Indicators is necessary but not sufficient, because the emotional climate of the organization has a huge effect on the amount of positive or negative energy put into attaining the enterprise's goals. Regular monitoring of the 'soft' side of the enterprise is essential. I have already mentioned the Organizational Climate Survey which takes the ten key organizational variables, plus Vision, and gives a clear indication in figures and words of where people think the organization is currently on each dimension, and where they would like it to be. These highlight the key issues and so enable the board to focus its managers on crucial organizational blockages.

Milestone event-namely, the completion of:	Assumptions to be tested
1. Initial data search and preliminary feasibility analysis	4: 1993 world OEM market 8: Average OEM order size 9: Sales calls per OEM order 10: Sales calls per salesperson per day 11: Salespeople needed for 250 selling days per year 12: Annual salesperson's salary 13: Containers required per order 14: Shipping cost per container 16: Production days per year 18: Annual manufacturing worker's salary
2. Prototype batches produced	15: Quality to get customers to switch 19: Materials costs per disk
3. Technical testing by customers	3: Unit selling price 15: Quality to get customers to switch
4. Subcontracted production	19: Materials costs per disk
5. Sales of subcontracted production	1: Profit margin 2: Revenues 3: Unit selling price 8: Average OEM order size 9: Sales calls per OEM order 10: Sales calls per salesperson per day 12: Annual salesperson's salary 15: Quality to get customers to switch
6. Purchase of an existing plant	5: Fixed asset investment to sale 7: Effective life of equipment
7. Pilot production at purchased plant	6: Effective production capacity per line 16: Production days per year 17: Workers per production line per day 18: Annual manufacturing worker's salary 19: Materials costs per disk 20: Packaging costs per 10 disks
8. Competitor reaction	1: Profit margin 2: Revenues 3: Unit selling price
9. Product redesign	19: Materials costs per disk 20: Packaging costs per 10 disks
10. Major repricing analysis	1: Profit margin 2: Revenues 3: Unit selling price 4: 1993 world OEM market
11. Plant redesign	5: Fixed asset investment to sales 6: Effective production capacity per line 19: Materials costs per disk

Figure 16 Kao Corporation's Discovery-Driven Planning Process

HARVARD BUSINESS REVIEW July-August 1995

THE HUMAN RESOURCES

These key organizational variables from the Organizational Climate Survey – adaptability; work quality; clarity of personal responsibilities; financial rewards; non-financial rewards; organizational clarity; personal performance indicators; group performance indicators; learning climate; and leadership – are crucial to the board's Supervision of Management. They need to be measured annually, unless the environment is very turbulent in which case they should be measured more often, but not so frequently that you risk killing what you have planted by continually digging up the roots to look at how it is growing.

From this data one can determine the 'discriminating questions' for the board to pursue for each variable. These are the questions to ask of managers about their work and its connectedness to the total development of the enterprise. No dimension should be allowed to become the province of one specialist function alone – they must all maintain links with their internal customers.

I have used the same Organizational Climate Surveys with customers as well as staff and have been pleasantly surprised at the correlation between the two sets of views.

Another frequently used management performance indicator is the Staff Attitude Survey. These are often undertaken regularly by the personnel, or human resources, function and can be useful if handled properly. Sadly, few are. My experience is that they often demand only simple single-point (just one tick) responses, rather than differential responses (logging where you are and where you want to be) which do not give the measured difference between where a person thinks the organization is and ideally where they would like it to be, and therefore do not give helpful direction by creating a positive emotional climate to drive the enterprise forward.

The management of people is a line manager's role, not a personnel, or human resources, function. These can act as a coordinating agency, but it needs to be built into the job description of line managers that they collect the data on their people – length of time with the company; length of time in a particular job; levels of competence attained; sickness rates; absenteeism rates; turnover rates, and so on. From these figures a complete picture within each work unit, and across the organization, can be built up for presentation to the board to give a clear picture of the trendlines in the underlying emotional climate and performance of their organization. The board then commissions a People Development Strategy Audit which results in a broad picture of the effective deployment of staff needed to achieve the Purpose of the organization.

CUSTOMER PERCEPTION PERFORMANCE INDICATORS

New work is under way on codifying and measuring customer perceptions and this too can inform a board better of the 'soft' side of the enterprise's performance. Customer perceptions are a key indicator for Supervising Management as they provide crucial information on the external perception of the enterprise and therefore its potential to retain and develop premium-paying customers.

Effective customer satisfaction systems can be paper-driven and inexpensive, although high-tech examples are beginning to multiply. Sadly they are often not treated seriously by the board or line managers, and can easily become the province of a beleaguered customer services group who have a lot of vital information for the organization, but no system for disseminating it, so that its value is lost.

In the 1990s, brand names have come under great pressure from legal 'clones' and 'own brand' labels taking significant market shares. The fightback by the brand names has been intriguing: some have begun to use the new information technologies to get much closer to their customers – what is called 'real-time marketing'. Some methods are relatively low-tech. Philips of Eindhoven took

vans full of industrial designers, anthropologists, cognitive psychol-
ogists and sociologists around the Netherlands, Italy and France to
brainstorm ideas and listen to customers' developing needs for their
new on-line children's product. From this data they developed the
product and ensured continuous feedback by sending more van
loads of staff to visit actual and potential users. The board does
not need the detailed results, just the overall project management
data to assure them that they are making a wise investment both
in their products and in their internal feedback systems.

More high-tech approaches have been taken elsewhere using
faxes, Freephone telephone numbers or the World Wide Web, for
instance, as two-way communications systems with their customers.
The customer queries are carefully codified and then studied with
the explicit intention of learning through focusing and refining that
product or service. In this way the board can ensure that the use
of its scarce development resources is as close as possible to the
real-time needs of its customers and so, hopefully, retain them or
acquire new ones.

Apple Computer codifies information from its hot line calls, and
its Customer Service folk interact via the telephone or e-mail to tell
customers about new products and services. From this they can
easily identify and codify for the board's use the top ten customer
issues each week. This information is then fed to the design function
so that they can improve new releases and project future customer
needs.

Early on Apple learned, to their concern, that many customers
thought that the 'mouse' was a foot-pedal and had great difficulty
getting it to work. Although the instruction books were clear, people
were not necessarily reading them, so they decided to build the
solution into the computer itself. This 'software welcome mat'
appears as soon as you switch on the computer and introduces
people to the basic system.

Kellogg does its 'real-time marketing' by putting Freephone
numbers on its food packets to encourage its customers to telephone

about nutritional issues. It gets invaluable dialogue about how and when its foods are used and in what quantities. Levi Strauss has started a women's made-to-order service in the US. Sales clerks measure customers and feed the data into an on-line information system. They let customers try sample jeans in the same store to ensure the right fit. The information system is linked to a cutting machine and the jeans are made to order at just $10 more. The data they collect on their customers during this process is invaluable.

Ford and other car manufacturers are moving towards such made-to-order systems. Benetton of Italy has for some years used a system of on-line cash tills which send information back to Bologna to track changing customer tastes. They can see what their customers are buying, where, and in what styles and colours. They hold most of their stock in Bologna in grey and have perfected a core competence of rapid dyeing-to-order and distribution processes. Such systems can even work in the defence industries. During the Falklands War the Westland Helicopter Company had computerized its production planning system to the extent that as the overnight battle and logistical reports came in from the military commanders the company was able to flex its manufacturing and maintenance capabilities to give priority to the most desperately needed items.

All these examples illustrate the validity of the 'moments of truth' comments mentioned earlier, and the growing recognition of the need to convince customers through price and product or service quality that you give 'good value for money'.

Risk Control

Behind the key performance indicators and the overseeing of management performance systems is the basic notion that the board needs to be able to know where the company is and where it should be so that deviations can be assessed and resources wisely allocated to correct the situation. Otherwise it is taking unnecessary risk.

Risk is essential to an enterprise. If we had full knowledge of the future there would be no risk. But we live in a gloriously imperfect world that allows for great rewards, harsh punishments and major disasters. Most convergent, binary thinkers are trained to screen out risk. For activities that are concerned with public health and safety that is fine. But for other business activities it leads to narrow perspectives, unimaginative futures and a rotting head.

The Cadbury Report on the Financial Aspects of Corporate Governance[28] recommends that the directors make statements in the company's annual report and accounts on the 'effectiveness of their internal systems of control' as a way of assessing risk for shareholders. It was assumed that this was already high on most boards' agendas, whether of listed or unlisted companies. In my experience it is not and boards often take unnecessary risks because they do not have sufficient reporting systems, even though they are encouraged to have an Audit Committee of the board.

Gerry Acher, Head of Audit and Accounting for KPMG, says, 'Some companies, large and small, have established an attitude of mind throughout the organization that [the control system] gives it strength and resilience on which it can rely. In other cases internal controls are looked on simply as the type of machinery which can be relied on to work without much attention.'[29] He stresses that such control systems should stretch far beyond the purely financial, particularly the monitoring of expenditure, and must go into production or service quality, health and safety at work, training and monitoring systems for employees, and security systems – the security of people and physical and intellectual property. All these are aspects of a growing directoral discipline – 'corporate risk management' – which tries to reduce risks, particularly through the use of 'what if . . . ?' scenarios. Corporate risk management is the ultimate responsibility of the board.

In the end boards still tend to return to the assessing of financial risk as the highest priority for the enterprise's and board's survival. One increasingly used technique by financial analysts is the 'Z-score'. Ratios appropriate to the enterprise are selected, weighted and then added together to produce a single index. Whilst there is no single model, a typical Z-score would comprise at least:

Profitability
Working capital
Financial risk
Liquidity.

To derive Z-scores you need to use key balance sheet figures with the profit and loss account to get a measure of the company's health and risk exposure. If, like Queens Moat House Hotels in 1991, the Z-score is negative, then the company is at risk as it has a profile similar to failing, or failed, businesses. This financial distress can lead to different outcomes. In the UK in recent years we have seen the well-publicized cases of Maxwell Communications Corporation (administration outcome), Pentos (receivership), Queens Moat Houses (capital reconstruction), British Aerospace (rescue rights issue) or Tiphook (major disposals) to illustrate the point.[30]

Professor Richard Taffler of the City University Business School, London, says that of the 152 bankruptcies of fully listed industrial companies in the UK until December 1994 only two had positive Z-scores based on their last accounts before failure, and of the other two he says not even Z-scores can see through apparent fraud. Yet not all companies with low or negative Z-scores will fail.

A development of the technique known as 'risk rating' uses a company's Z-score history to predict the probability of financial distress for such negatively scored companies. Taffler reinforces the Supervising Management message: 'that plotting corporate performance over time [means that] problems can be picked up before the Z-score goes negative, giving more time for appropriate action to be taken'.

It is essential for directors and boards to sustain the 'helicopter view' when dealing with Supervising Management. A powerful example is the way in which Marks & Spencer keeps an overview of its strategic resources, as shown below, through assessing tangible and intangible resources, to ensure its continuing competitive advantages:

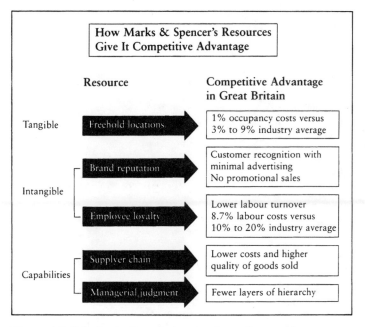

Figure 17 Marks & Spencer's overview of strategic resources

Any company that attains that level of clarity deserves to be a brand leader.

CHAPTER • 6

Accountability

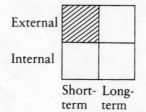

Organizational efficiency: Short-term, externally-oriented thinking

Accountability is both the simplest and most complex of the board's tasks.

All over the world the media is fixated by the lack of competence, unreliability, untrustworthiness and sheer greed of directors. There are plenty of examples to draw from and the mixture of fraud, corporate collapses, political or economic scandals related to companies, cronyism, graft, and nepotism to be found in the US, UK, France, Germany, Japan, Italy, Spain, Australia, Hong Kong or China, to name just a few, are sufficient to keep the media fuelled for many years to come.

I suspect that this seeming lack of accountability has always existed but that now we are much better informed about it. However, the issue is that boards have now got to be much clearer about their values and ethics and more aware of, and skilful in their use of, the new media technologies to be openly accountable. This demands a more holistic approach by the board to the range of accountability issues, in particular the board's quality of thinking, its ethics and values, its obedience to the law and the consistency of its behaviours to its stakeholders define its approach to accountability. It is a huge challenge, and likely to be debated widely as we enter the twenty-first century.

Traditionally, the first duty of a board and a director, especially in common-law based countries, is to the company itself as a legal personality. This is rarely understood by directors yet it is embodied in law in most countries. As few boards have effective induction processes this simple point is often missed. But it has key implications for the accountability of the board, and its collective and individual responsibilities and liabilities. Most directors, however, see themselves as 'representatives' of internal or external factions – specialist functions, the shareholders or lenders – so the implications of this prime duty to the company often passes them by.

I am frequently surprised by two reactions when I mention this fact. The first is to deny it, then to insist that either executive, or non-executive, directors 'do not count' in this case. Each wishes to believe that they are exempt from some or all accountability. In almost all common-law countries the distinction between 'executive' and 'non-executive' directors is not recognized: a 'director', of whatever type, is a director. This can come as quite a shock to those who 'hold themselves out to be a director' by having, for example, the word 'director' on their business card or notepaper. By so doing they can become potentially as liable as anyone formally on the board, and the scope of those liabilities is huge. This has caused a great deal of concern amongst, for example, financial services companies. In the 1980s everyone strove to have the word 'director' on their business card 'because it is important to get clients'. As their liabilities became clearer in the nervous 1990s most have insisted that it is removed from their card and job title.

The second reaction, on recovering from the truth about their range of liabilities, is to believe firmly that they are covered by 'limited liability'. This, again, proves the paucity of their induction programme. Limited liability in most countries is granted to the owners, the shareholders, up to the limit of their paid-up shareholding. The directors are *not* covered by limited liability, unless they have some shareholding. Even then that is the only part that is covered. After that they may then resort to their indemnity insurance cover, but that is often riddled with exceptions.

All in all, being accountable is an awesome set of responsibilities for the board collectively and for the individual directors. In the UK there are at least four hundred laws which define the director's responsibilities and liabilities. Most of them are way beyond what most boards would describe as their business. As a result of directors having no self-regulating professional body, they are not covered by the precedents of civil and criminal law. What is alarming is that the number of director-orientated laws is growing rapidly as politicians ride on the back of justifiable public anger over the directoral behaviours headlined in the media. Such headlines give a highly distorted view of the ethics and behaviours of the vast majority of directors. My experience around the world shows me that most boards have surprisingly high ethical standards and are working at long-term relationships with their stakeholders – but that is boring news for the media.

The Global Pressure for Corporate Accountability

I have not attempted a comprehensive review but have focused on those nations where the issues, and possible solutions, are being actively pursued.

The United Kingdom

The UK has become a world leader in the reform of corporate governance. Whether this has been intentional is open to debate. The main event which propelled Britain to the front of the debate was the publication of the Cadbury Report on the Financial Aspects of Corporate Governance in 1993. It strongly recommends *voluntary* procedures and behaviours that boards should follow to improve *shareholders'* understanding of and control over the company's finances. It also reviews other aspects of the ways in which companies are governed, including the role of the independent non-executive director, and the design of executive directors' remuneration packages. The latter led to the publication in July 1995 of the Greenbury Report on the remuneration issue, including directors' pensions.

The Cadbury Report's most effective recommendation has been the splitting of the chairman and chief executive roles, which in the UK at least has now become almost *de rigueur*.

From 1995 there will be a review by the sponsors – the Financial Reporting Council, the London International Stock Exchange, the Institute of Chartered Accountants in England and Wales, the Confederation of British Industry, and the Institute of Directors – of the extent of voluntary compliance by listed boards prior to setting up 'Cadbury Mark 2' – in late 1995 this was announced as the

Hampel Committee. In the background lurk dissatisfied share-holders and stakeholders, and politicians who would like to see a mandatory approach being imposed on boards' accountability.

The strictly 'governance' issues, board structure and composition, and its financial responsibilities and liabilities, have tended to be underplayed in the furore over excessive director pay rises, bonuses and stock options – particularly in the recently privatized UK indus-tries. Ironically, many UK boards have been mirroring the old trades union game of claiming the 'going rate' to keep their pay differen-tials, and then trying to ensure that they are in the upper quartile regardless of their organization's performance or the risk of exposure. Many shareholders want Greenbury and especially Ham-pel to address executive director remuneration more effectively.

However, it is not just the establishment of Audit, Nomination or Remuneration Committees, or balancing the numbers of execu-tive and independent directors, about which we must concern our-selves. The pressure for change which the original Cadbury report has unleashed now looks unstoppable, and it is not just the small shareholders and outraged members of the public who are squeal-ing. The UK's National Association of Pension Funds wants to see the maximum term of directors' 'service' contracts shortened from the present three years to a maximum of one, and a retirement age of seventy for listed companies. They think that this would answer accusations about the present 'old boys' network' renewing the service contract of an underperforming executive director, then sacking him or her so that they can collect the rest of their service contract as compensation. It wants 'reciprocal arrangements' addressed, especially for non-executive directors sitting on each other's boards and approving each other's remuneration packages.

It also wants shareholders to have better access to the terms of directors' contracts. Even the more cautious Association of British Insurers insists that the 'relevant aspects' of any director's contract and the rationale of pay awards are fully disclosed. In the wider world there are public rumblings about using US-style proxy campaign statements and quarterly reporting to shareholders to make transparent directors' total benefits packages.

Within just two years the results of the Cadbury Committee recommendations are already being felt, despite its 'voluntary' nature. The general feeling is that, although the changes have been relatively small, they are growing and are moving in the right direction. Sir Malcom Smith, chairman of W.H. Smith, announced that of the nineteen Cadbury recommendations, they have already installed seventeen. It moved swiftly to install a Nominations Committee for new directors, largely comprised of independent directors. One of the great innovations of Cadbury, and a useful precedent that should be demanded by *all* executive directors, especially of subsidiary companies, is the creation of a final procedure through which independent directors can seek independent professional advice if they feel uncertain about an executive board decision. The Institute of Directors, London, already offers such a legal service for its members as part of a wider legal advice service.

There is some concern that Cadbury has already gone too far too quickly. The London Stock Exchange has rather wimpishly proposed that listed companies no longer be required to spell out compliance with Cadbury. This flies in the face of rising global shareholder and stakeholder power and their demands for more 'transparency' in board decisions and subsequent accounting. But even the London Stock Exchange wants two parts of the voluntary code as a requirement for all listed companies – that the auditors certify that the company is a going concern; and that the directors certify that their internal controls are adequate.

The role of the independent 'non-executive' director is still being questioned by many executives. However, they are seen by many shareholders and stakeholders as a key element in the process of identifying, and if necessary sacking, ineffective executive directors. This puts independent directors in an interesting and potentially powerful position. It is obviously meant to deal with Lord Halifax's famous dictum – 'the problem with British companies is that they

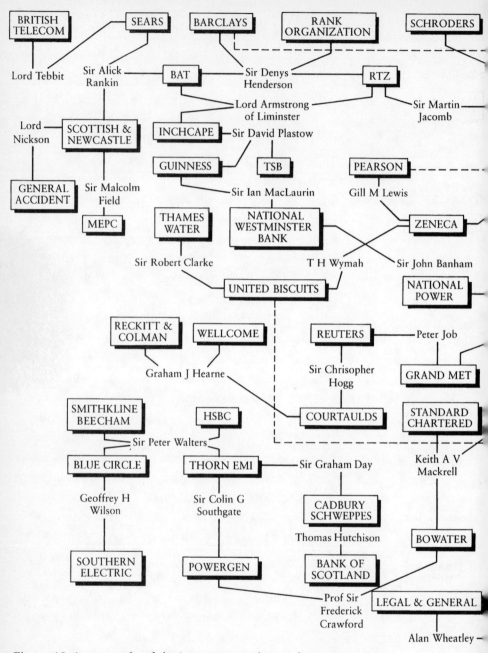

Figure 18 An example of the interconnectedness of non-executive directors in the UK, March 1995

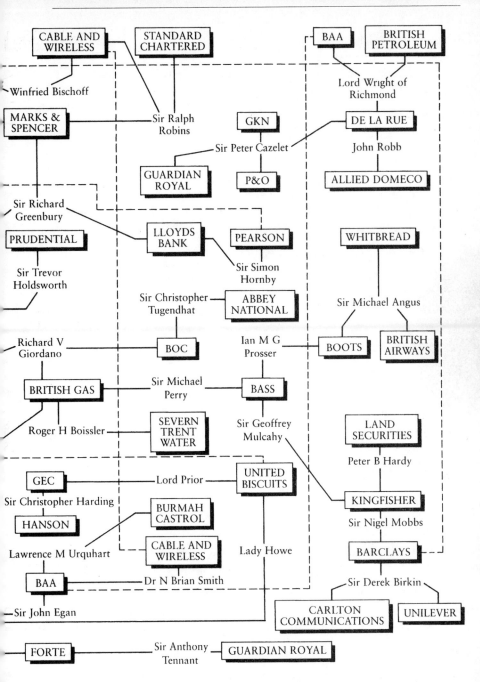

Source: PIRC using latest published accounts

mark their own exam papers'. Which brings us back to the effectiveness, training, motivation and rewards of the executive directors.

The Greenbury Committee, headed by Sir Richard Greenbury, Chairman of Marks & Spencer, says little about effectiveness or training. The main recommendation is that directors should be engaged on one-year contracts and that *shareholders* should have the right to approve all new performance and other bonuses and pension schemes. It has watered down its original recommendation to say 'boards should take into account employees' pay rates' when considering their own. This will do little to damp down the current public disquiet with director remuneration. Greenbury stresses the need for self-regulation by the directors rather than creating new legislation. Its main recommendations are on full disclosure of the processes of directors' pay setting and their comparative levels.

Arthur Andersen, a management consultant, published a study in August 1995 showing early compliance to the Greenbury recommendations. The privatized energy companies were best: on average, fifty percent were compliant with twelve of the committee's recommendations, which are likely to be incorporated into the stock exchange rules. Privatized water companies ranked third with twenty-seven percent compliance, pharmaceuticals with nineteen percent, manufacturing industry sixteen percent, and the financial services industry ranked worst with only thirteen percent compliance.

The average level of compliance is only thirty-one percent and no company surveyed had one hundred percent. The Greenbury recommendation that remuneration committees are comprised only of non-executive directors is met by fifty-seven percent of companies. Only six percent disclose how, and by whom, non-executive salaries are set; and only sixteen percent of companies give the comparator group of companies used to help determine director's pay. As Brian Freedman, the partner in charge of Andersen's compensation and benefits package, said, 'Many major businesses have some considerable way to go before they have covered the "Greenbury gap".'

The accountability debate is bound to continue in the UK and abroad until such eminent bodies look beyond pay to individual, and board, effectiveness in relation to all four tasks of the board.

One particular characteristic of the UK corporate governance debate is that it is running in parallel with a similar debate in the public sector. The creation of many new government agencies and corporations, and of National Health Service Trusts, has created over ten thousand new director jobs. The Institute of Directors in London is beginning to address this, and the publication of their *Standards for NHS Boards* and the Audit Commission's *Take On Board* are a good start.

The issue of ineffective corporate governance is not confined to the UK. Increasingly questions are being asked around the world about the nature of board effectiveness.

The United States of America

In the United States the corporate governance debate has a different flavour, but its ends are similar to the UK – to ensure that boards, directors, presidents and CEOs are more openly and rigorously accountable to the shareholders and stakeholders. I can see in my mind's eye the annual general meeting addressed by Gordon Gekko in the film *Wall Street* when he strides late into the packed extraordinary general meeting. There are serried ranks of executives on the platform giving out their usual coded EGM-speak. He marches down the aisle demanding to be heard and, turning to the audience, denounces the executives' performance, shouting to the shareholders, '*They* do not own the company, *you* do!' Tumultuous applause follows, and on a vote he wins his point. I feel that this vignette gives an idea of the temperature of the corporate governance issue in the US – the conflict between the power of entrenched executive directors and the seemingly disenfranchised shareholders.

Curiously, independent directors now outnumber executives significantly on US listed company boards. Over seventy-five percent of US chairmen combine that job with that of the chief executive, in contradiction to growing practice in the UK. Shareholders have demanded that boards of directors hold executive management accountable for poor performance. Recent examples of those ousted for alleged poor performance include the chief executive officers of General Motors, Kodak, American Express and Westinghouse. In the US in the 1990s it seems that board oversight is replacing hostile takeovers as a discipline on poorly performing companies.

Many US companies have been working on eliminating directors whose interests conflict with their 'independent' business judgements. Unlike many continental European and Asian boards, in the US some sixty percent had no directors representing leading customers or suppliers, nor had significant connections to the company's management, according to the Conference Board.[31]

Top management is also reluctantly loosening its control of the director nomination process through the growing acceptance of the need for a Board Nomination Committee, as in the UK. The Conference Board notes that only six percent of US-listed companies had one in 1973; now sixty-four percent do. More than ninety percent now have a Compensation Committee, against sixty-nine percent in 1973.

The fight to split the chairman and CEO role will be a long one, unlike the UK. The Conference Board points out that it is in the US 'a clearly established pattern', an *expectation* of a CEO on taking a corporate leadership role. It does not comment, except indirectly, on the unhealthiness of combining the roles and so concentrating such power in one individual, but this probably explains the underperformance of many of the great US corporations during the 1980s and 1990s.

The Conference Board reports how time is spent on the US board:

25% median on strategic issues
21% median on financial control
20% median on operations control
34% median on committees and other duties

It also says that forty-four percent of manufacturing industry directors are 'very diligent' in preparing for meetings, thirty-nine percent are so in non-financial services companies, but only thirty-four percent prepare diligently for financial service board activities.

Underlying much of the US thinking has been a book published in 1933 by Adolph Berle and Gardiner Means – *The Modern Corporation and Private Property*.[32] This argues that in the Darwinian struggle for survival the American public company is the winner because of its reliance on the largely unfettered power of strong managers and the existence of small, fragmented shareholders weakened by their own inability to coordinate. Berle and Means stated that if the shareholders did not like the use and abuse of such managerial power they could sell. This structure is seen as far outweighing in efficiency the costs that it incurs. One can still hear these arguments strongly in New York, London, Frankfurt, Hong Kong or Tokyo today. But you can also hear a counter-argument beginning to rumble. In part this is coming from disenchanted small shareholders, and large pension and institutional fund managers, who are beginning to appreciate the possibilities of using the new information systems to 'coordinate' themselves in Berle's and Means' terms. There is growing evidence of shareholders' alternative policies and strategies being published through the media, and the use of the new information technologies to coordinate the collection of proxy votes to challenge the executives' decisions. The growing role of the powerful Calpers (Californian Public Employees Retirement Scheme) and non-profit organizations like Institutional Shareholder Services Inc. is highly significant here.

It should also be remembered that US politics has traditionally been against big institutional shareholdings. Big insurers and banks have been banned from this, the latter under the Glass-Steagall Act. From 1940 mutual funds were discouraged from getting deeply involved in corporate governance, and in the 1980s many state anti-takeover laws blocked leveraged buy-outs. Part of the counter-argument in the US is to allow big shareholders such as mutual and pension funds greater freedom to experiment with different ways of overseeing management performance. Institutional ownership has grown dramatically during the 1980s and 1990s. This is mainly as the result of the rapid growth of pension funds and mutual funds. Institutional investors now own about half of the equity of the largest 1,000 US companies, and in many cases it is not unusual for the institutional ownership to exceed seventy percent. High shareholding levels have encouraged US institutional investors to become more active in wanting to oversee the performance and conformance of these enterprises.

US courts are becoming tougher on company directors and boards. Although Delaware is a tiny state, more than half of the US's largest companies are incorporated there. This means that Delaware corporate law is virtually the equivalent of national law with respect to the larger corporations and needs, therefore, constant monitoring to see which way the US corporate governance wind is blowing. An interesting example is seen in the Delaware Supreme Court opinions on *Cede and Co.* v. *Technicolor Inc. and Paramount Communications Inc. and QVC Network Inc.*; and *Kelman* v. *Lynch Communication Systems Inc.* In each case the defendants were members of a board whose company had agreed an acquisition by a favoured buyer, despite shareholder protests. The Delaware Supreme Court had some very harsh words for directors whose decisions were not seen as fully independent.

Japan

Because of the interlocking nature of Japanese big business and finance, small Japanese shareholders have very limited rights. The only channel to express their views is the Annual General Meeting, but this is almost impossible to use both because of the formal process of the meeting, which keeps the executives firmly in charge, and the use by the board of *yakuza*, criminal gangs who 'police' the meetings and put down any dissent. Only the *yakuza* are allowed to cause trouble, and they can be stopped if they are properly paid.

Japanese Annual General Meetings have three main functions. First, to endorse formally the nomination for board members and auditors. Second, to determine the board's remuneration package (which is usually significantly below that of the Anglo-Saxons). Third, to approve the financial reports – although comparatively limited financial information is offered. Exceptional issues, such as a merger, will need the consensus of shareholders, but they are not allowed to vote on any topic related to the management structure of the enterprise. In theory shareholders can replace board members, but this would be very unusual in such a consensual and shame-based culture. They can also enter into special contractual arrangements between shareholders and members of the board, especially the president.

More than ninety percent of all listed corporations with a March accounting date (more than 1,200) hold their AGMs on the same day, often at the same hour. It is surprising if the meeting lasts more than thirty minutes. The notion of 'shareholder democracy' and 'shareholder power' does not exist within the web of overlapping industrial and financial interests. This is Japanese corporate governance's greatest weakness as bad decisions, like the rush to invest in property in the 1980s and early 1990s, not only cause problems on a single company's balance sheet but also have disastrous national knock-on effects for the banks and other financial institutions. This, in turn, affects non-listed companies seeking finance. It also illustrates the emotional climate in many Japanese corporations where there is a strong belief that the major corporations actually belong to the *employees*, not the shareholders, because the employees devote their whole life to a single corporation, whilst shareholders can 'vote' by buying or selling their shares. The fact that these shares, as in many parts of Asia, are frequently diluted by the executives through rights issues is not deemed important.

Even in Japan there are signs of a growing unease with the way that corporate governance – structures, processes, responsibilities and liabilities – is going. On 9 August 1993 Akira Suzuki, a former director of the Janome sewing machine company, went to the Tokyo District Court and filed a suit on behalf of his old employer which seeks 1.5 billion in US dollars in damages from twenty-nine of the company's former and current executives. Japan's commercial code has been amended to allow affordable law suits. He is a trend-setter. His company had been the target of a well-documented greenmail attempt by a later convicted extortionist, Mitsuhiro Kotani, and the company had been in trouble ever since. The lawsuit alleges that the Saitama Bank loaned the money through an affiliated financial company to Janome, who passed it to Kotani's Koshin Group. The case is pending but it does show a possible way forward in Japan. However, the underlying mindset is still against change. In 1993 it was reported that both Nomura and Daiwa blocked demands by such powerful investors as California's Public Employees Retirement Scheme when it suggested that the appointment of independent directors might help avoid future scandals.

Germany

Germany has been seen as a model of enlightened corporate governance since its restructuring after the Second World War. But the German two-tier board system is now under growing criticism. Failures and problems that have emerged in the last five years in cases such as Schneider, Metallgesellschaft, Volkswagen, Daimler Benz, DASA, Adam Opel and others have strengthened the call for reconsideration. The main question is, 'How can this type of thing happen with a two-tier board, the high calibre of management on those boards, and the quality of the (usually interlocked) shareholders?' I suspect that the issue is not so much the structure but the perennial problems of powerful personalities, overlapping shareholdings, and lending which leads to the corruption of the two-tier ideals.

To illustrate the point, sixty percent of Metallgesellschaft's shares are owned by the biggest names in Germany – Deutsche Bank, Dresdener Bank, Allianz Insurance and Daimler Benz. In addition the Emir of Kuwait is a major shareholder. One would have expected better from the executives. The German corporate governance design is based on having two separate boards – a supervisory board, *aufsichtstrat*, and overseeing the performance of the management board, *vorstand*. The latter ensures that the employees and other stakeholders can be informed of the company's position and aspirations. The supervisory board allocates capital and labour, with the chairman exercising a casting vote if necessary. It is responsible for appointing executive managers and debating and agreeing strategic issues. The second-tier management board then runs the day-to-day operations of the enterprise.

The growing criticisms of the German two-tier system are not only of the structure but of the potentially over-cosy relationships between the supervisory board and management in human terms. A particular concern is over who supervises the supervisors. This has been the line of Gunter Ogger, who wrote the bestseller *Nieten in Nadelstreifen* (*Nitwits in Pinstripes*). He argues that although formally controlled by the shareholders, the interlocking ownership and funding interests of the major shareholders tends to mean that they are accountable only to themselves. As German executives have not faced redundancy through hostile takeovers and the consequent public criticism, the cosiness is reinforced.

In the Metallgesellschaft (MG) failure the board members were a list of the great and the good in Germany. They are all good managers yet they failed to *oversee* the complexity of affairs – MG had 258 subsidiaries generating some DM27 billion of annual turnover. Some reports partly put the blame on the Chairman of the Supervisory Board, Ronaldo Schmitz, head of corporate finance at Deutsche Bank. He is a financial expert, and seen by others as personally cool. His appointment in 1993 was seen as a counterbalance to the then CEO, Heinz Schimmelbusch, who had a reputation for elaborate and risky business diversification strategies. Press reports said that Schmitz put great pressure on Schimmelbusch to sell off loss-making subsidiaries and start a process of rationalization. Only when this started would Schimmelbusch's five-year contract be renewed. It is reported that he did not know of the losses on the oil-trading side which later triggered the main collapse. It was later that Schimmelbusch walked between the two corporate headquarters to tell Schmitz of the problems that had become horribly clear, and then rapid action was taken. In a fortnight Schimmelbusch and his colleagues were ousted, but the board 'conformance' issues of Management Supervision and Accountability were not resolved so easily.

The Supervisory Board failed to identify that the lack of managerial controls, and the supervision of that management, put the whole of MG at risk. It was not necessarily a personal failure by the board members but a systems failure of the corporate governance system. The interlocked commercial interests allowed both sets of board members to be much less critical of the powerful CEO's authoritarian style and his expansionist ideas, especially as they were being *funded* by some of the very same shareholder/directors.

In August 1995 the Organization for Economic Co-operation and Development (OECD) published a critical report on Germany's 'relations-based' corporate governance system, claiming that it will block development of innovative, knowledge-based, high-tech industries and the creation of new companies in the formerly communist East Germany. They argued for the increased use of stock market finance, more risk capital, and the wider availability of lending from non-bank sources. Interestingly, the OECD report believes 'certain tensions and evolutionary trends' could lead to a convergence of the German and Anglo-Saxon systems of corporate governance and financing for the following reasons:

- The internationalization of individual companies and the economy in general could prompt changes to information and accounting policies as foreign investors become more active in Germany, and German companies use their increased scope to secure finance abroad.
- Increased internationalization of regulatory standards could also promote change.
- Promoting business in East Germany and the financing needs of the new knowledge-based companies, with heavy investment in intangible capital, will require financing methods other than those relying on traditional bank demands for collateral.
- Institutional forms of saving could come to play a more significant role.

France

France has been suffering growing business corruption problems at very high national levels, as Table 4 (overleaf) shows, and some fear that it could become another Italy if the new Chirac government is not careful. A recent *Le Monde* survey suggested that two-thirds of French company chairmen believe French business to be riddled with corruption. More than half of these bosses said that they would welcome an anti-corruption purge along the lines of Italy. The size of the problem is disputed. A previous prime minister, Edouard Balladur, had appointed 'three wise men' to organize an inquiry into corruption in French business. The charging of Bernard Tapie seems to have been the start of this national process.

In response a group of senior French executives has called for a series of corporate governance reforms and criticized strongly the typical cross-shareholdings of many of France's largest companies. This Viénot Committee, similar in its role to the UK's Cadbury Committee, has been created by the Patronat, the employer's federation, and the AFEP, the association of French private companies. It has called for tougher measures to remedy the inexperience of

Table 4 Trouble at the top in the French business world

Martin Bouygues	Managing director of Groupe Bouygues	Charged on December 22nd with misuse of corporate funds to win public contracts.
Guy Delouany	Managing director, Compagnie Générale des Eaux	Charged in May with corrupt practices in securing a public water contract.
Paul-Louis Halley	Managing director of Promodès, the second largest French retailing group	Charged in September with fraud and corruption regarding corporate bribes for supermarket planning permission.
Patrick Le Lay	Head of TF1, the largest private television channel (owned by Bouygues)	Detained for 36 hours in November for questioning about alleged bribes to secure the exclusive transmission rights to the weekly national lottery draw.
André Lévy-Lang	Head of Paribas, a large investment bank	Charged in December with falsifying group accounts.
Louis Schweitzer	Chairman of Renault	Charged on January 2nd in connection with an illegal phone-tapping scandal in the mid-1980s when chief of staff to Laurent Fabius, then prime minister.
Pierre Suard	Managing director of Alcatel Alsthom, the world's largest telecommunications equipment supplier	Charged in March with corruption and fraud in over-billing France Télécom. Banned from exercising his corporate functions while charges are pending.
Bernard Tapie	Former centre-left government minister and former owner of Marseilles football club	Sentenced in November to eight months' imprisonment and five years' ineligibility for public office for match-rigging. Appeal pending. Facing four more corruption charges.

Source: The Economist[33]

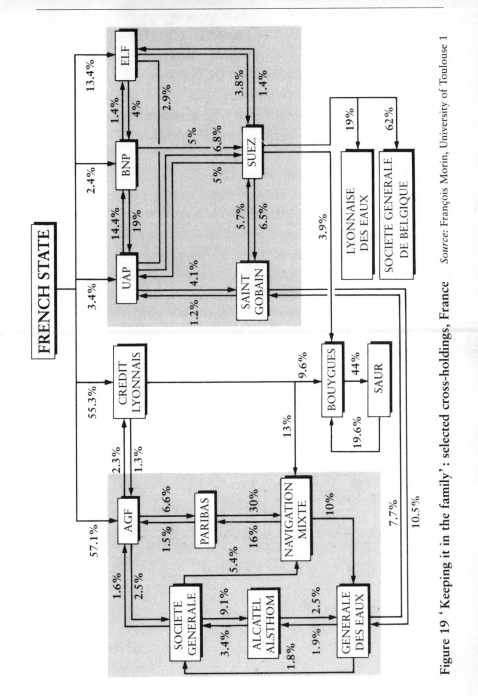

Figure 19 'Keeping it in the family': selected cross-holdings, France   *Source:* François Morin, University of Toulouse 1

boards and, thereby, reduce the potential for conflicts of interests. There is growing evidence that directors do not reflect shareholders' interests.

Marc Viénot, Chairman of Société General, has said that the French cross-shareholding system is 'undesirable' as many of France's major companies hold significant chunks of each other's shares, as shown in Figure 19 (p.139). This is adequately demonstrated in Suez, the premier French industrial and financial holding company which is now riven by divisions amongst its biggest shareholders – Saint Gobain, Elf Aquitaine, and Union des Assurances de Paris. Monsieur Viénot wants boards to set up audit, remuneration and nomination committees; to ensure that directors do not sit on more than five boards; and have a minimum of two directors independent of the company, clients or shareholders. They must put the company's interests first.   The French government has replied supporting the ideas and saying that it will reveal a similar set of guidelines for the large *public* sector. They think that corporate governance is a matter for the companies and the markets, not government legislation. Monsieur Viénot agrees: he does not want compulsory legislation.

Hong Kong

Hong Kong has been tracking the UK's experience of the Cadbury Committee recommendations, but has two other aspects to contend with in its rumbustious markets – the rapid growth and internationalization of local, usually family-owned, companies; and the Chinese dimension – specifically the influence it currently has on the nascent stock markets in Shenzhen and Shanghai, coupled with the growing rivalry with Shanghai for becoming the premier financial centre for China.

Hong Kong has a similar regulatory regime as the United Kingdom. The Securities and Futures Commission (SFC) is independent of the Stock Exchange, although they do liaise, and self-regulation is increasingly encouraged. Until the last few years corporate governance has not been treated very seriously in Hong Kong, but now that companies are becoming more complex, and are listed nationally and internationally, the roles of the board and directors are becoming important. This importance is also being recognized in public and semi-public enterprises.

The key issues being addressed in Hong Kong are:

- Stopping directors having 'paper' board meetings and ensuring that they are now physically present and that informed discussions and decision-making happen.
- Stopping directors in a controlling position in listed companies voting themselves salaries disproportionate to their profits and prospects and so abusing the dividends of minority shareholders.
- Ensuring that in Hong Kong the listing rules which require that every publicly listed company has two non-executive directors is obeyed. These directors should not be related by business, relationship or any other means to the other full-time executive shareholding directors.

  This is very difficult to achieve as so many directors sit on interconnected boards. One way around this, recommended by the Hong Kong Stock Exchange, is for non-executives to be appointed for a specific period, which is disclosed in the Annual Report and Accounts. The implication, and desire of the stock exchange, is that every non-executive should give sufficient time to the affairs of the issuer and should not accept the appointment if he or she cannot. As many Hong Kong non-executive directors have over twenty directorships this is a real problem.
- Ermano Pascuitto has been appointed to review Hong Kong Company Law. A Consultative Document has been issued outlining the problems. Prominent among them is the fact that Hong Kong company law is nineteenth-century in origin and was only brought into line with the UK Companies Act of 1947 in 1973. At that time

there were some 26,000 companies on the Companies register. In 1995 there are over 150,000. Given current changes in corporate legislation and the hand-back to China in July 1997 (which is introducing its own company law modernization proposals), the need to consolidate and simplify Hong Kong company law is urgent; although, at least in theory, under the international treaty signed between Britain and China the present Hong Kong laws and ways of life will be respected until AD 2047.

- The issue of family control and the relationship of directors to family-dominated boards is only just beginning to be addressed. The argument for separating the chairman and chief executive roles is not fully appreciated. This is largely due to lack of training. The introduction of the IOD Diploma in 1993 is beginning to have a positive effect on this understanding through the voluntary training of the next generation of Hong Kong directors.

- The internationalization of Hong Kong means that there are now many regional headquarters and subsidiaries of international businesses present. Many of their practices are governed by legislation in their home country, which can cause conflict locally. Added to this are the effects of China's economic revolution and the rapid development of neighbouring countries: Hong Kong has had a continuing level of high inflation, and many of its neighbours are relatively high risk economies. Investors are, therefore, wary of making further investments until both political and economic risks are more quantifiable.

- The management style of Hong Kong is not British but a hybrid of its neighbours. To understand the board attitudes and processes it is best to know the nationality of the parent, or dominant shareholder, and how long it has been present in Asia. This is the prime challenge of people trying to encourage corporate governance in Hong Kong.

Australia

Corporate governance in Australia has been a pretty rough and ready affair over the last decade. The tensions are between the focus of a young and growing economy on entrepreneurism come what may, and a growing concern about the need to regulate the more questionable behaviours of a small, often interlocking, group of very powerful businessmen. As the power figures of the 1980s – Alan Bond, John Elliott, Christopher Skase, Abe Goldberg and so on – give way to a slightly more considered approach in the mid-1990s, there seems to be a growing awareness that corporate governance can never be the same again. There are two main reasons for this, one legal, one financial.

The event which has caused most comment amongst Australian boards of directors in recent years has been the majority verdict in the New South Wales Court of Appeal in the *Deloitte* v. *AWA* case. AWA had sought damages against Deloitte for failing to detect losses in foreign exchange trading by the company's dealer. Mr Justice Rogers found, amongst other things, that if the *executive* directors of a company were negligent then the company could be liable for a proportion of the damages arising in cases involving auditor negligence. Therefore, executive directors had an additional need to exercise due diligence in conducting a company's affairs. By contrast Mr Justice Rogers found that *non-executive* directors were responsible only for overall policy and corporate governance. They were entitled to rely on the 'judgement, information and advice' of senior executives on the day-to-day operations of the company. But the Appeal Court *reversed* this finding, stating that 'A person who accepts the office of director of a company undertakes the responsibility of ensuring that he understands the nature of the duty a director is called upon to perform . . . As the law of negligence has developed, no satisfactory policy ground survives for excluding directors from the general requirement that they exercise reasonable care in the exercise of their office.'

Given the nature of case-law, this finding has enormous implications for corporate governance in the Commonwealth countries, and has transformed the thinking of Australian boards – they realize that the 'cowboy days' of the 1980s are over. There has been strong criticism that many of the deals of that time had questionable ethics (and were not noticeable for making money either). Now the mood in Australian boards may have swung too far the other way with directors being rather intimidated by the AWA judgement and tending towards overcaution rather than facing the risks necessary to business. The grounds under which Australian directors can plead ignorance of their operational world have been heavily curtailed.

The second pressure driving change in Australia is the growing power of the fund managers, especially the superannuation fund managers. At the time of writing there is a great debate about the need to restructure the membership of the Coles Myer boards where some of the members are being subject to public scrutiny and attack. The sudden publicity surrounding previously faceless fund managers reflects their growing power around the world. In Australia they have drawn the wrath of Prime Minister Keating, who has called them 'donkeys' following their pressure to reform the Coles Myer board, and on Pacific Dunlop to sell off their food division. Willingly or not, they are becoming the guardians of corporate ethics.

Ethical issues, or more correctly 'stakeholder' issues, are also becoming more openly discussed in Australia. In a country whose natural resources revolve around extraction industries, agriculture and tourism, public awareness of physical environmental issues and concerns over Aboriginal rights are beginning to change the mindsets of some boards. At the time of writing, BHP were under heavy criticism for their alleged polluting of the Ok Tedi River in Papua New Guinea.

These major pressures for change are helping to redefine the role of the Australian Institute of Company Directors. As with the Institute of Directors in London, the AICD is beginning to emphasize the educational and 'competence' needs of directors. This is likely to take things down the track of eventual self-regulation once appropriate educational and assessment processes are in place. Graham Stubington, Chief Executive of the AICD, says that the changes are under way. As an example he quotes the fact that 95 percent of member companies now have separate non-executive chairman and chief executive roles. A recent Korn Ferry consultants study of both large and small Australian companies found that such job separation was now the case in 80 percent of their sample, and a growing trend.

The problem, then, is how do you find suitable people to become directors? The easy solutions of appointing accountants, lawyers or executives from other companies is not usually satisfactory – their appointment is no guarantee that they know about *directing*, as the AWA finding has highlighted. Graham Stubington points out that this is a growing problem since over the next decade some 25 percent of Australian directors will retire, mostly because they are too old. This makes the education and accreditation of the next generation a key issue. Two new initiatives have shown the way ahead. The creation of ProNED, a training programme for non-executive directors, will ensure the supply is of better quality, and is a promising start. But to help the reframing of the thinking and behaviour of Australian boards the AICD has produced a Code of Conduct with the following eleven rules:

1. A director must act honestly, in good faith and in the best interests of the whole company.
2. A director has a duty to use due care and diligence in fulfilling the functions of office and exercising the powers attached to that office.
3. A director must use the powers of office for a proper purpose, in the best interests of the company as a whole.
4. A director must recognize that the primary responsibility is to the company's shareholders as a whole but should, where appropriate, have regard for the interests of all stakeholders in the company.

5. A director must not make improper use of information acquired as a director.

6. A director must not take improper advantage of his position as a director.

7. A director must not allow personal interests, or the interests of any associated person, to conflict with the interests of the company.

8. A director has an obligation to be independent in judgement and actions and to take all reasonable steps to be satisfied as to the soundness of the decisions of the board.

9. Confidential information received by a director in the course of the exercise of directoral duties remains the property of the company from which it was obtained and it is improper to disclose it, or allow it to be disclosed, unless the disclosure has been authorized by the person from whom the information is provided, or is required by law.

10. A director should not engage in conduct likely to bring discredit upon the company.

11. A director has an obligation, at all times, to comply with the spirit as well as the letter of the law and with the principles of this Code.

Another way forward, suggests Mr Justice Rogers, is to have the roles and tasks of the board and its directors spelled out in the Memorandum and Articles of Association of the company.

New Zealand

New Zealand has been the model for economic and social revolution amongst the 'Anglo-Saxon' nations during the late 1980s and 1990s. The effects of the 'Rogernomics' approach and the subsequent dismantling of much of the machinery of the state, coupled with the acceptance of export-led growth, has changed the old cosy way of corporate life. One of the effects has been the rise of people who can make a career out of being a truly independent (non-executive) director.

Two major forces for change in New Zealand corporate governance since 1990 have been:

- The growing number of Parliamentary Acts which directly affect directors
- The privatization and corporatization of the government sector

The following Acts exemplify the significant increase in board and director responsibilities and liabilities:

Companies Act 1993
Resources Management Act 1991
Building Act 1991
Health and Safety in Employment Act 1992
Privacy Act 1993
Fair Trading Act 1986
Commerce Act 1986
Financial Reporting Act 1993.

Recent New Zealand governments have moved non-core activities out of the public sector, either by creating a corporation, for example in the areas of Health or Energy, or by privatizing them, for example Telecom and New Zealand Rail. As a result some two hundred companies have been established which, in turn, has created about 1,600 new director positions. All these appointments are of non-executive directors.

The New Zealand economy has been one of the world success stories in the recession, with an improvement in GDP and decreases in inflation and unemployment. There has, however, been a slight slowdown in the development of the private sector, as the focus has been on privatization, corporatization and the effects of the Western recession on New Zealand. Whilst the number of

Table 5   Growth of registered companies in New Zealand 1985–93

Number of registered companies in New Zealand on 31 March

1985	128,636
1989	160,370
1993	162,652

Demand for capital:
Year ended 31 March

	No. of floats	Total capital sought ($million)
1991	11	1,536
1992	11	479
1993	28	1,164
1994	12	550

Table 6   Board size and fees in New Zealand 1995

Average size of board	9
Average no. of board meetings per annum	10
Average duration of board meetings	4 hrs
Women directors in large companies	9.2%
Average fees (NZ$):	
Non-executive chairman	28,343
Deputy chair	22,511
Director	17,955

* *Source:* IOD/Price Waterhouse Fee Survey 1995

registered companies has grown, the demand for capital has dropped off (see Table 5, above).

A key issue in New Zealand in 1995 has been takeovers. The 1993 Act required a panel to be appointed and for them to recommend a code on takeovers. This was produced for the minister in mid–1995. In the event the Government decided not to implement it 'meantime'. This is causing considerable debate in New Zealand corporate governance circles.

New Zealand enjoys high standards of corporate governance compared with other parts of the world (see Table 6, opposite).

The low level of directors' fees is causing concern in New Zealand's corporate governance circles. However, the annualized fee increase reported by 104 participating organizations in the survey was 11.7 percent. One quarter of participating organizations reported increases of more than 25 percent – a similar pattern to 1994 when a significant realignment occurred.

Some of the specific characteristics of New Zealand corporate governance are:

- Executive chairmen are abnormal in large companies
- The majority of the board are non-executive directors in large companies
- Audit committees have been the norm in New Zealand in large companies for many years
- There is a growing trend towards boards having operating plans and objectives
- Evaluation of individual board member performance is undertaken regularly in many of the larger companies
- Training for directors, particularly for non-executive directors, is widely undertaken

The training courses run by the New Zealand Institute of Directors in Wellington are of a high quality and are attracting a growing number of directors, not just from the large companies but also from the Maori community.

Across the world an argument seems to be emerging for something similar to the coherence of the UK's 'unitary board' model, although national pride may not admit it. The key elements seem to be the push for more transparency for shareholders and other stakeholders through such ideas as:

- A balanced number of executive and truly 'independent' directors

- Short-term contracts for directors, with openness about the process and transparency of the detail of remuneration and pension packages
- Split chairman and chief executive roles
- Audit, nomination and remuneration committees of the board
- Increased accountability to all shareholders
- Increased accountability to the 'stakeholders'
- Appraisal of both board and individual director performance

If a board anywhere in the world can achieve these ideals, then they are well on the way to becoming both a performing and a Learning Board.

The Board's Responsibilities

Let us now look at each group on the list of 'stakeholders' in an enterprise to see how the accountability debate is affecting the power balances on a board, and what can be learned from these changes.

Because of the great focus in the current corporate governance debate on the role and rights of the shareholders, we need to look at them not just in terms of corporate governance but also in terms of their aspirations and growing legal rights. These rights are becoming increasingly clear in common law countries and stand in sharp contrast to many directors' views of their shareholders, so aptly described by John Galsworthy:

> And now Old Jolyon [Forsyte] rose to present the accounts. Veiling under a Jove-like serenity that perpetual antagonism deep-seated in the bosom of a director towards his shareholders, he faced them calmly.[34]

SHAREHOLDERS

It is the shareholders who own the company, not the executives, although sometimes this is difficult to see. In some family and professional businesses they may be one and the same, but the growth in the size of enterprises around the world usually ensures that over time they become distinct. The board's, and each director's, prime duty is for the stewardship of the company itself as a legal personality. Secondly it is responsible to the shareholders, and, finally, to the 'stakeholders' (even the IOD's *Standards* makes only an indirect reference to them as 'other interested parties').

With sufficient votes most shareholders can unseat a board, change a remuneration system, alter policies and strategies, and insist upon greater accountability. They rarely do. This is in part because small shareholders are so fragmented that the only viable option they have to show their feelings about the board is to buy or sell the shares. The modern major shareholders, the financial institutions, feel similarly. They have traditionally not intervened in corporate governance issues within a company and have expressed their opinions solely by buying or selling the shares.

However, investors have finally begun to focus on questions about the assessment of the *effectiveness* of boards. If ways can be found to measure and improve board effectiveness, then many investors feel that a more positive cash-stream and profits will follow. They believe that this will help counter the continuing media exposure of fallibility, corruption and downright directoral incompetence around the world.

On my many travels I often test the IOD findings that 92.4 percent of directors have had no training or development for their directoral role. These figures have never been disputed when related to directors in France, Germany, Catalonia, Sweden, the US, Australia, New Zealand, Hong Kong, Malaysia, Brunei or the Arabian Gulf. Only once were they challenged strongly by a director of a UK defence company, but not on the grounds that they were untrue; rather that the truth would unsettle the staff and the stock markets. I am sure he is right, but it looks as though that will be a necessary price to pay to correct matters for the twenty-first century.

Shareholder Value

The lack of training means that it is often very difficult for directors to focus on shareholders' needs. Such needs can range from the very simple – to ensure that their investment is safe and producing a reasonable return, that the directors are carrying out their fiduciary duty – to quite complex: increasing shareholder value.

The techniques for this are many. Most fall into one of two main camps, Market Value Added, or Economic Value Added. Market

Value Added (MVA) looks at the difference between the enterprise's market value and its accounting book value, after adjusting for various accounting issues which do not reflect current economic reality. Economic Value Added (EVA) is the internal method of measuring corporate performance closely associated with MVA, and is trademarked by the US consultancy Stern Stewart.

More than a hundred companies have adopted this rigorous approach so that executives and shareholders can better understand performance measurement and incentive compensation. This latter is important as it shows a greater clarity of the executives' ability to increase shareholder value, even if the EVA is negative but improving. EVA also insists wisely that only one-third of a bonus declared is paid in the current year. The other two-thirds are in a deferred bonus account and subject to loss if the change in the next two years is negative.

What interests me is the great gains in share prices of the companies with EVA. They have gained at three times the rate of the market as a whole. In the US Coca-Cola and Briggs & Stratton shares have quadrupled in value over the past five years. Fletcher Challenge in New Zealand, and Murray & Roberts in South Africa, have doubled in the past year. Quaker Oats of Chicago now has a premium price/earning ratio in its industry. Merrill Lynch analysts give EVA as one reason to buy and sell.

All ways of measuring increasing shareholder value focus the board on the *stewardship* of the scarce resources and the corporate performance from them, linked to incentive schemes of many sorts.

Shareholder Democracy

In the US and UK there is also a drive towards more 'shareholder democracy' as both a political and economic force for social stability and development. In Singapore one can even buy up to US$33,000 worth of shares a day from automatic teller machines – a symbol of the true shareholding nation. But many small shareholders are puzzled and angry by the obvious lack of true 'democracy' in the companies in which they hold shares when they come to comment and vote on board performance. A typical example is a letter in the London *Times* from Cynthia Walton:[35]

> Sir, As a novice attender at a shareholders' meeting I went to the AGM of Midlands Electricity in Birmingham. MEB became a quoted company in 1990 and the chairman was fulsome in self-congratulation about progress since then. He reported a handshake of around £360,000 to an outgoing managing director who left before his three-year contract expired. However, a questioner was able to show that the full farewell pay-off package was around £1.1 million including pensions, potential options etc. and subsequently suggested that directors should not be appointed on three-year contracts but on one-year contracts, to avoid such pay-offs in future.
>
> There were over 1,000 people present. However, when questioned, the chairman admitted having received in excess of 87 million proxy votes which would allow all the resolutions put to the meeting to be adopted. What a sham! The meeting was asked to show its support of one-year contracts by voting against the re-election of the board members and numerous orange voting cards were waved in the air. But of course to no avail.

This mishandling of the emotional climate, especially for small shareholders, is found right across the world. In East Asia it is a common shareholder complaint that the directors act as if they are the owners (in many cases they are still the majority shareholders) and that they disregard the shareholder constituency to which the board is ultimately responsible. A typical complaint of the small shareholder is that executives take decisions, especially on rights issues, which frequently dilute their shareholdings.

The Shareholder Fightback

There is, inevitably, a growing shareholder fightback which any board monitoring changes in its external environment should view seriously. The institutional investors, especially the insurers and pension funds, are taking a more active interest not just in the financial performance of the business, but also in the quality of its direction as well as its management. This means looking at both the quality of intra-board relationships and their strategic thinking capabilities. Increasingly the public performances of board members, especially via the media, are also noted. This is not a plea for 'media training' for directors, even if some directors' TV performances make John Major look like Superman. Media training may help a little. The real improvement in relations with shareholders will come from building consistently high quality dialogue with them.

A growing part of the shareholder fightback is playing the board at its own game by using proxy votes at AGMs or EGMs. This is happening in the US where, through the use of the explosion in provision of public media and new information systems like the InterNet, it is becoming much cheaper to broadcast alternative ideas, policies, strategies and information about a company, regardless of the board's position. The implications of these currently weak signals seem to have been missed by many boards. The baby is not just beginning to cry but looks as though it will howl the house down in the early twenty-first century. Even then some boards will not hear.

The basic process for shareholder proxy building campaigns is to find a group of intelligently naive, committed individuals, or institutional funds, to produce alternative analyses of the firm's figures, then produce alternative policies and strategies and recommendations for board membership to take the enterprise forward into a healthier future. These ideas are then publicized locally, regionally, or nationally through the press, radio, TV if it can be afforded, and the InterNet. The proxies are sent to a central point where they are counted and then taken to the AGM or EGM, the debate and the final vote. These mini-Gordon Gekkos may finally be getting a bit more of their own way. Some US boards I know are beginning to pay attention. A few non-profit organizations, like Institutional Shareholder Services Inc., are helping such shareholder proxy schemes become much more effective.

A leading force in shareholder activism is the California Public Employees Retirement Scheme (Calpers), a large institutional investor with US$80 billion under management. Calpers has had remarkable success in getting their, and other, shareholder voices heard, the ideas debated and their ideas on corporate governance installed. It has not been easy and they are not always listened to, but they have growing clout. Overseas directors should pay attention as Calpers is about to track foreign boards, particularly in the UK, Germany, and Japan. James Burton, Chief Executive of Calpers, told the International Monetary Conference in June 1995 that Calpers planned an overseas company starting in October 1995. It would mirror its US activities – discussions with companies in which it has shares, and which are performing poorly, to improve directoral and managerial performance. He said that they had targeted thirty-five companies in 1995 on the list it calls its 'Failing 50' – the worst performing companies in the 1,200 in which it has large amounts of equity. Calpers holds thirteen percent of its assets overseas and expects this to rise to around twenty percent in five years.

Significantly, Burton has already had talks with European funds which were seeking a more active approach, but he said he was looking for 'something a little more comprehensive', about which he would not be more specific. A strong 'weak signal' if ever there was one for listed companies.

This move is likely to accelerate shareholder activism in Europe. Already companies like the Prudential and RailPen are demanding a bigger say in corporate governance. There are other well-publicized examples. The performance of the Union Bank of Switzerland has been put under pressure by BK Vision, a fund management group, and in the UK the highly-publicized shareholder criticism of Saatchi & Saatchi led to the resignation of the chairman, Maurice Saatchi. Whether the resulting company, Cordiant, will perform better is a question of great debate as it has now lost some of its long-standing clients to 'New Saatchi'.

But whatever the immediate outcome, the general message for boards is clear – neglect your shareholders at your peril.

The Rise of the 'Stakeholders'

It is a given on most boards around the world that their prime, indeed their only, responsibility is to their shareholders. Viewed through the lens of the Companies Acts this may seem strictly true, but if one thinks for even a minute about the number of laws *outside* the Companies Acts, or their overseas equivalents, which a director must obey then it becomes daunting. In the UK there are over four hundred laws affecting directors, and very few of these relate to shareholders. Most relate to a diverse group of external interests with whom the company interacts – the 'stakeholders'. Like it or not, the board and individual directors are increasingly required to take a much wider view of their responsibilities under the law for the many other groups which give them their energy niches in society. All demand some form of homage and control. This is going to make the board's life much more complicated in future. Policy Formulation and Accountability are becoming more openly political as many of these groups have societal change or single interest foci with which the directors will need to learn to cope.

Critics will immediately complain that this is grossly unfair because unless directors focus only on the shareholder they cannot do their job properly – their energies would be dispersed over too wide an horizon. This is true, but not a sufficient argument. Directors *cannot* operate outside the law, even if most of them do not know what laws they should be obeying.

The term stakeholder is still an amorphous idea, but an enquiry by the Royal Society of Arts, Manufactures and Commerce, published in London in July 1995 as *Tomorrow's Company*, will have an impact on the positive acceptance by boards of the notion that it is an important part of their externally-orientated role to create good stakeholder relations. They are increasingly held accountable to them in so many ways.

A basic list would include:

Shareholders
Regulators
Legislators
Customers
Employees
Suppliers
The Physical Environment
The Local Community

It is a daunting list, but let me stress that in *all* of these areas there are laws which set the coordinates for board accountability and liability. There will be many more to come as politicians jump on a bandwagon which is popular with the public and does not involve raising taxes – the increasing restraint of the power of boards of directors.

CUSTOMERS

Product quality, reliability, design for purpose, delivery guarantees, assured maintenance, warranties and customer's charters are all ideas used increasingly by boards to create that vital perception of 'good value for money' in the customer's mind which ensures that the enterprise grows within its chosen market niches.

Learning Boards must ensure two key aspects of customer accountability. First, that the appropriate authority is properly delegated to their managers; that the managers, in turn, imbue a 'task and quality culture' throughout the customer-facing side of the organization; and that the appropriate ratios and trendlines are built into the supervising management system so that the board is informed of the consequences of its strategic decisions and can learn from them. Second, that the board has the ultimate responsibility for the overall *perception* of the enterprise by the customer. This involves getting involved in commenting and debating in public – something for which many directors are woefully unprepared, particularly in the event of product problems and disasters. Problems have been so numerous that the legislators have moved in with a vengeance and made boards' lives much more difficult. The US has a raft of product legislation designed to protect the consumer and ensure that products or services offered to the public are fit for their purpose. This has had many positive benefits on the design and reliability of products. However, the courts have been giving such high compensation and damages awards for allegedly faulty products that boards believe it is not worth carrying on in that business, especially as no insurer will be willing to cover them. This nearly finished the US light aircraft industry when the damages awarded after people had crashed light planes reached such levels that the manufacturers decided to up sticks and go home. It was not good news for importers either as they are subject to the same laws.

A similar process has been eroding the European Union manufacturers over the last ten years. Here the law cases have been fought out not just in the civil courts but also in the criminal courts. Most boards are unaware of these new EU laws, but from October 1994 they have included not just products but many categories of services provision as well. For example, they extend consumer protection and product safety regulations to *second-hand* goods, which are now expected to perform as well as new – no matter how illogical that may sound. Already a Warrington, UK, supplier of second-hand white goods has been driven into insolvency after a strict enforcement of this new law in Spain. The law also allows for a general recall of goods sold, with all the attendant publicity, if a recurrent fault is found – failing that prosecution is possible. A European Union-wide database on products is being established as part of a trans-EU monitoring system. Criminal sanctions include three months imprisonment for guilty *directors* and senior managers, and fines of up to £5,000 on summary conviction – and that is only from the lower courts, and for second-hand goods! Do not tell me that we should 'only' concern ourselves with thinking about the company and its shareholders. This legislation-driven accountability by boards for customers and products is still growing rapidly and needs strategic reframing.

However, boards have an unhappy knack of shooting themselves in both feet through faulty products or services, and sometimes going for their head as well, egged on by their PR departments.

Such self-induced public relations disasters are forever with us. Taking a few just from the second six months in 1994 as an example, Cunard had its flagship *QE II* refitted in a German yard on a very tight schedule. Inevitably a project of this size and complexity did not run smoothly so by the time the ship arrived in Southampton for its much publicized Christmas 1994 cruise it was still full of fitters, electricians and plumbers trying to get things up to Cunard's publicly perceived very high standards. There was little flexibility in their schedule so a large number of powerful, and potentially litigious, customers, were bumped off the cruise – with no warning, no immediate redress, and no sympathetic handling. The cruise started across the winter Atlantic with many, seasick, fitters still on board. In New York where the ship was due to collect more powerful and litigious customers, the port authorities stopped its further progress because of safety regulations infringements. They were unhappy about the fire-fighting and egress facilities. Eventually some customers had their Christmas cruise in the Caribbean. The story was headline news in the press and TV on both sides of the Atlantic throughout the Christmas holiday with dreadful consequences for Cunard's image in customers' minds. There was an apparent lack of contingency planning on such a high risk project, and its directors seemed arrogant when initially interviewed on TV. It was a case-study example of how not to be seen as accountable to customers as stakeholders.

Intel suffered a similar fate over the much-heralded launch of its Pentium computer chip. When faults were found in the chip the line taken by senior executives was, 'Well, it's only a problem for real mathematicians and scientists as it only affects really big numbers.' When it was pointed out in the press that such numbers could be critical for aircraft navigation and air traffic control systems, more waffling occurred. This worried the general public and panicked the PC users, who almost certainly would not have encountered the problem but whose confidence in the reliability of the new chip was now shaken severely. Eventually a product recall happened and Intel joined the list of businesses humbled by an insufficient sensitivity to their accountability to their customers.

Around the same time Unilever had to admit that its revolutionary detergent 'Persil Power' (also 'Omo Power') was defective. Its arch rival, Procter & Gamble, had been saying for months that it damaged certain types of common clothing on repeated high temperature washes. As the European detergent market alone is valued at some £6 billion a year this was a major blow to Unilever. At last, after initial denials and obfuscation, it admitted a cover-up. 'We made a mistake. We launched a product which had a defect we had not detected,' said Mr Morris Tabaksblat, co-chairman of the Unilever Consumer Products group. 'I think that we were very enthusiastic about an exciting new product ... and did not look closely enough at the negatives. Somewhere between research and marketing, something went wrong ... under the normal pressure to be first to the market.'[36] The new detergent contained a manganese catalyst 'accelerator' which reacted badly to certain dyes in extreme conditions. A new formula has been launched, and it sounds as if a major lesson was learned.

One can understand any board's early reactions to bad news – a blend of 'we do not want to hear this' plus 'we are not like that, we're good people'. This early denial is a classic example of the 'cover-up' attitude and behaviours learned from our earliest days. It is an example of 'groupthink' – the ability of a group to convince themselves that whatever they do is by definition right, so that any external information that contradicts their decisions is wrong.

It is extraordinarily easy for a board to self-censor itself. If the board is already 'cloned', or a club-type, then it is almost inevitable. This is the main argument for independent directors – who will ask discriminating questions and pursue them relentlessly so as to protect the shareholders and other stakeholders against the self-censored assumptions of the executives. Chris Argyris deals with this in his book *Knowledge in Action*[37] where he says that most of our counter-productive organizational behaviours come from learning in our earliest days how to cover up mistakes, and then cover up the cover-up. Once this is learned as an effective behaviour it is transferred everywhere, and becomes such a habit that we do not even acknowledge such behaviours exist within us. It becomes 'undiscussable'. Many boards operate in the same way. Mike Dixon of the *Financial Times* has added Argyris's Archetype to his growing list of *The Laws of Organizational Stupidity* – the more threatening a problem is to those responsible for solving it, the deeper it will become engrained under ramifying levels of camouflage. It is against this that Learning Boards must be fighting.

However, it is not just products which concern customers. They have values and lifestyles which change. Unless the board is continually sensing and monitoring the external environment, such changes can easily be missed. Some happen fast, as in the fashion industry or management consulting, and those involved have to learn to live with and learn from such risks. Other well-established industries become so self-censoring that it is difficult to discuss the issue of their long-term viability *at all* at board level.

The West and Japan both have mainly ageing populations. Consequently the demands for more individualization and inter-action with products and services, or the idea of pursuing prevention rather than cure, and the idea of needing to control the impact of our civilization on the physical environment all highlight medium- and long-term warning signals for many apparently well-established industries. They also signal opportunities for others. The list below, devised by me to challenge the strategic thinking of boards and focus debate (and therefore by no means comprehensive), gives examples of energy niches that might change:

Cigarette manufacture
Red meat production
Dairy products manufacture
Chemicals manufacture (man-made)
Pharmaceuticals manufacture (man-made)
Paper production
Car and truck manufacturing
Petroleum fuels production
Plastics manufacturing
Alcoholic spirit production
Deep-sea fishing
Nuclear electricity production
Forest products manufacturing
Sugar production
Office furniture manufacturing
Commercial property retailing
Book publishing
Acid battery manufacturing

Can you imagine a world with much smaller or even no supplies of these? To survive we may need to learn to, as people's values and fashions change. We may need to come up with, for instance, better designs, more environmentally friendly materials and production methods, and more sensitive ways of dealing with the millions of people displaced from these industries as we evolve new ones.

The changing customer perception of the meat industry is an interesting example. The 'production' process can be shown televisually as appallingly inhumane from start to finish. Yet many people eat meat, either out of habit, for nutritional purposes, or because they like it. Indeed, in parts of East Asia the rise in meat consumption is noticeable. This is not surprising as a traditional greeting in China is, 'Have you eaten?', reflecting the long history of hunger. Rising affluence will trigger a search for better quality and more diverse food. Within that search meat production will play an important role in East Asia and, later, Africa and South America. But its popularity, especially 'red' meat's, is dropping in the Western world.

How do you handle the dilemma if you are a meat producer's board? Playing on the benefits and being honest about the downside is a good start. So it comes as a shock to me to see the way in which McDonald's, a fast-food chain, is handling a libel case in the UK. Two unemployed defendants are being taken through the courts by McDonald's in reportedly the largest and most expensive libel case in British legal history. The defendants distributed a pamphlet accusing McDonald's of a range of undesirable actions, including ravaging the world's rain forests, polluting customers, polluting the environment, and underpaying staff. McDonald's strongly refute these charges. However, the resulting publicity has not helped the public perception of McDonald's. The public and press can easily sympathize with two unemployed underdogs up against a huge multinational. The publicity surrounding the case appears to have exposed McDonald's to the very charges about which they are most sensitive. A lot more information has been generated about its low pay policies, production and quality for the public domain. Its own evidence on animal husbandry and subliminal advertising techniques has dented its 'good neighbour' image. They have also acknowledged that in the UK the annual staff turnover is almost two hundred percent. At the time of publication, there has been no adjudication of the issue.

Libel actions are very dangerous tools for boards, especially if there is any sniff of 'groupthink' around for the media to work on. Moreover, they are a good technique for customers and other stakeholders to get more information, and ultimately accountability, from a board.

EMPLOYEES

The Creation of 'Intellectual Property'

Putting 'employees' under the stakeholder title seems to me an entirely reasonable step. They risk a different type of investment from shareholders and customers – their employment and income – but in today's turbulent world it is a personal risk much bigger than that of most shareholders. They are also a key resource of the organization. Their ideas, learning and energy determine ultimately whether strategies and tactics will succeed and to what quality goods or services will be delivered. They control the 'know how' and 'know why' of the enterprise. If committed they can implement change rapidly. They can also hold back progress through dinosaur-like intransigence, malicious obedience, or uninformed enthusiasm.

Until I became a company director I had thought that it was a condition of the Companies Act that each chairman had to put in their annual report and accounts the phrase 'Our people are our greatest asset'. If this is so, where do I find people on the balance sheet? I will admit that in a very few companies they do put key players there – in football teams, software houses and advertising agencies – but this is very tough for the accountants as the 'asset' has a brain and legs and can simply walk out.

There is another aspect to valuing people as assets which boards should consider seriously – their learning. This may sound at first like another 'soft' idea. It is not. It is a very hard-edged one indeed. The question is how can an organization capture its learning in a rigorous and regular manner? There are simple well tried and tested ways for the operations folk. Budgeting five minutes per day at the start or end of a work period to ask, 'What went right?', 'What went wrong?', and 'What are we doing OK?', then logging it, is a key line manager's role. Action Learning groups tackle key issues in a cross-disciplinary way. Then there are 'town meetings', 'hot groups', and formal debates. In all these cases the trick is to be systematic in *codifying* the learning and then ensuring that it is moved to where it is needed. Such codified feedback sets up the conditions for asset creation because a legal right can be created over it.

Although the world's perception of the Uruguay Round of the General Agreement on Tariffs and Trade (GATT, now the World Trade Organization) was generally of a massive row over agricultural subsidies in the US and EU, the less newsworthy early agreements had behind them a radical notion – that the majority of wealth creation in the twenty-first century would come not simply from the ability to manufacture but from the ability to create and use the knowledge, attitudes and skills of the employees – their 'know how' and 'know why' – and the board's investment in that. The argument is that the ability to mass manufacture, and to a lesser extent the ability to deliver service, is likely to follow the cheapest labour around the world. So only core competencies are worth defending strongly. The rest can eventually be 'outsourced'.

As organizations follow what Charles Handy has called the 'shamrock organization type'[38] – a strong organizational core of full-time employees with the board at its hub, then 'leaves' of out-sourced services, part-time and job-share staff, self-employed workers and consultants, and project-based contract groups – the need to integrate these diverse learning sources increases. All these people have the capacity to learn. If this is properly recorded and protected, then the investment in that learning can become a *legal* asset – the *intellectual property rights* of the enterprise. These can then be valued and placed on the balance sheet.

The Uruguay Round recognized that intellectual property was one of the *future* bases for world trade and has ensured that corporations can create legal rights over their learning. These intellectual property rights (IPRs) will be of key significance as assets on the balance sheet. The generally-accepted international categorization of intellectual property rights are in the creation and registration of:

Patent
Copyright
Registered Design
Trademark
Servicemark

In many legislations there are 'trade secrets' and 'design rights' categories.

Viewing them you will notice that they are all manifestations of an enterprise's investment in *learning at work* – the essence of the Learning Organization is in adding value in this way.

PATENT

Patent is slow to acquire but very powerful once you have it. It is easily transferred to the balance sheet in most legislations, where it should remain for years. Whilst relatively expensive to police, it is usually easy to enforce as the courts give it a high status. The main problems, as in all IPR protection, come from emerging countries, like China, which, despite signing the international conventions, have little cash and an attitude that there should be no tax on knowledge. Life as a patent agent or lawyer can be demanding, especially as now the leading edge is moving away from inanimate objects and looking at the creation of patents over life forms. In genetic engineering, the 'onco-mouse' is the first to be patented, and genetically engineered sheep and cows are coming. In November 1995 the US government took out a patent on the genetic make up of a Papua New Guinea tribesman who seems to be AIDS resistant. The ethics of this are highly debatable, particularly as the research begins to impinge on human beings, but the trends are clear enough. Life is made even more demanding for the patent lawyers in the US where the criterion for patent awards seems to be, crudely, that the first person to the patent office who can prove they had the idea first gets it, whilst in Europe, just as crudely, it is the first person to get to the patent office who can demonstrate an original idea.

COPYRIGHT

Copyright is a rapidly growing field. The press is full of stories of claims and counter-claims for mind-boggling sums between such giants as Microsoft, Intel, IBM, Fujitsu, Warner Brothers, Virgin, Disney and Thorn-EMI, all trying to protect their copyright over everything from chip design, through software products, to music rights and illegal CD copies. The creation of copyright is the very existence for many of the new style 'software' companies and the courts are slowly trying to catch up with the rapid advances in information technology which threaten to make IPRs a very tricky area to police.

How does your board handle copyright issues? How many of your own enterprises-generated software systems have you bothered to protect? Or have you taken, legally or illegally, copies from other companies' systems? Do you ever do an IPR audit to check what your staff are learning that needs protecting? Do you let your staff walk out with copies of your operating disks when they leave your employment? How do you know? How protected are your customer, or supplier, lists? These are all investments made by you which have the potential for IPR audit and protection.

REGISTERED DESIGN

Registered Design can be thought of in a similar way to copyright. To what extent are the physical objects we create registerable? Or are we copying from others and, if so, what is our legal basis for so doing? Are we putting sufficient investment into designing new products or new versions of existing products or services? What feedback systems do we have from customers both to ensure the continuing viability of our products, and to reduce the risk of new design faults?

TRADEMARK

Trademark is an obvious asset to an enterprise. Although not necessarily legally linked to 'brands', this is what the public perception of a trademark is. It is meant as a protection of both the customer and the company by being a guarantee of quality. The value, and valuing, of brands is disputed hotly in the accountancy profession, so it is debatable how to handle brands as an asset, and whether they should go on the balance sheet.

Whatever the rights and wrongs, there is little doubt that brands are having a tough time worldwide at present. 'Marlboro Friday' is etched on every brand manager's mind – one of the world's leading cigarette brands had to make a dramatic price cut to compete with the increasingly fashionable 'own brand' products of the major retailers. A current case is the growth of the Cott Corporation which specializes in creating own-brand items. This relatively unknown soft drinks bottler has been taken rapidly by its president, Dave Nichol, to a US$800 million annual turnover in 1995. It now supplies cola and other soft drinks to major retailers competing directly against Coke and Pepsi, both of whom have had to increase significantly their advertising budgets.

Cott now supplies over a hundred retailers on four continents. These include such giants as Wal-Mart in the US, Sainsbury in the UK, Promodes in France, and Ito-Yokado in Japan. Now they are reaching beyond the own label idea and have launched Virgin Cola, a regular brand, with Richard Branson's Virgin Group. In the UK Cott has some 27 percent of supermarket sales and has cut Coke's from 44 percent to 32 percent. Although brands may be having a tough time, Cott is now a powerful trademark in its own right.

SERVICEMARK

Servicemark is the service-orientated side of trademark. It is seen, for example, on the automatic teller machines at banks – 'Service Till', 'Cash Point', 'Speed Bank', 'ETC' and so on. This is a fast-growing aspect of IPRs.

What are your board's policies and strategies towards the capture of organizational learning, creation of intellectual property rights, and valuation of such learning?

Employee Legislation

A growing amount of legislation insists that the board protects their people for health and safety reasons, limits their hours and conditions of work, ensures proper payment for work done, gives employment rights, eases the pain of redundancy, and ensures that a decent pension is paid. All of this is seen as reasonable and necessary in a civilized country. However, the growing bulk of legislation, and the crippling of the board's freedom of action, brings legislation under heavy fire in the US, Europe and Japan. The argument is that there should be a block on any more legislation. Instead it should be cut back, simplified, and local conditions should be allowed to dictate the interpretation of what is possible at any given time within the boundaries of civilized behaviour.

The idea of a 'social chapter' in the European Union has been pursued openly for ten years by the then President, Mitterand, and the then Director-General of the European Commission, Jacques Delors.

They were both influenced heavily by an older centralist organiz-ational model of trades union power in consultation with employers' power through a highly centralized series of national agreements which would then be imposed across the whole of the EU. Regardless of the economic and political arguments, since the EU is the biggest cross-cultural experiment in history, significantly involving three of the major quadrants of Hoftsede's cross-cultural model, it is highly unlikely that such supra-national agreements will ever be accepted fully.

However, supertankers are slow to change their course so we must wait to see in which way the 'social contract' and employees' rights arguments work themselves out. Britain has used its 'opt out' of the Social Chapter, and I am sure that others will find the reality of the imposition too much for them. Full-blooded legislation pro-posed in line with the Social Chapter has operated in Belgium, for instance, for some time and the resulting labour inflexibility seems to have gone unnoticed by the European Commission, even though it is based in Brussels.

Trades Unions

European trades unions have suffered a significant loss of power in the last decade and the old model of trades union militancy seems to be left increasingly to developing nations.

Table 7   Breakdown of the UK's employment-age population, 1995

11.7%	unemployed
24.3%	part-time workers
13.0%	self-employed
7.0%	temporary workers
2.5%	home workers
1.7%	youth employment schemes
39.0%	full-time employed

Source: Dr John Lloyd, Cranfield Institute of Technology

British trades unions have suffered a huge loss in numbers and power since 1979 when Margaret Thatcher came to power – from some 13 million members to around 7.8 million in 1995. They are still seeking to regain their numbers and influence, but a look at the redistribution of the working population in 1995 does not give them much hope:

The intriguing point is that only 39 percent now have a 'proper job'. It does not look as though things will revert to the pre-1979 position. The UK trades unions tactics to regain some credibility are, therefore, to influence and use those areas of the EU voting system where there is majority, rather than consensus, voting. Specifically in relation to board accountability for staff issues, these are women's issues and health and safety issues. If the trades unions can define any of their concerns in the light of these two, then they can influence other countries to push the issues through by majority voting.

This is not to imply that Learning Boards should not pay attention to trades unions. Far from it. If boards really did behave as if they believed 'our people are our biggest asset', there might be little use for unions. But boards are human and fallible and need careful auditing on their use and abuse of their people. Employees still need ways of combining to ensure their rights and such improvements as they feel necessary. A modern trades union could define its new roles and tasks along such lines and make it clear that it was working *with* the board to pursue the common wealth and social equity – and the trades union itself could be held accountable for this.

SUPPLIERS

The relationship between an enterprise and its suppliers is always a dynamic one because of the changes in the balance of power resulting from gluts or shortages. Boards need to ensure that they have agreed procurement strategies so that in times of shortage they have sufficient supplies to feed their manufacturing process and to service their customers. In times of glut they need to ensure that the stock pile is low enough to get as tight a grip on costs as possible. Hence the rise in time-based supplier relationships, like 'Just In Time' (JIT) manufacturing deliveries. These are flexible delivery systems where the supplier holds stock at their premises, or has very rapid manufacturing systems, and delivers just when the customer needs it. The economic benefits in cost reduction are obvious, but it takes time to build the long-term relationship between buyer and supplier to ensure that it works continuously. JIT reduces the amount of risk to both sides and so is a crucial part of a board's general risk profiling process.

The alternative way of handling such risks is to always buy from the 'spot' markets, buying as closely as possible to the time of need. But this can lead to stock-outs, or stock hoarding issues, which can have bad effects on profitability. It is for the board to approve its procurement strategy as an integral part of its financial strategy and its risk profile, to ensure that it remains a Performing Board.

Another key aspect of the financial strategy which the board needs to agree is its approach to suppliers' cash flow. The need to pay suppliers on time, and thus reinforce the mutual relationship, is crucial. Sadly many Anglo-Saxon countries have a lax attitude here, and the UK has a particularly bad cavalier approach to honouring supplier contracts. It is seen as an easy way of balancing cash flows, and of getting free credit instead of paying within thirty days. New European Union proposals on thirty-day payments to suppliers, or having to pay penal interest on outstanding sums, should put paid to this.

THE PHYSICAL ENVIRONMENT –
'GREEN' ISSUES

Perhaps the incident which had the biggest impact on world opinion about directors' duties in relation to the physical environment was the Bhopal chemical plant disaster. A gas leak in the Union Carbide plant on 3 December 1984 killed more than three thousand people and left thousands permanently disabled. Bhopal became a landmark legal case in establishing liability for hazardous industries in developing countries. It also raised the notion of including 'green issues' in the thinking processes of boards.

In September 1994 Union Carbide was forced to sell all its Indian assets for £60 million to McLeod Russell India. The Union Carbide 59.9 percent stake in their Indian subsidiary was sold to the highest bidder in a closed auction ordered by the Indian Supreme Court as part of the punishment given to Union Carbide for its part in the disaster. Sir Ian Percival, court-appointed receiver for the bids, and a trustee of the Bhopal Hospital trust, said in September 1994 that the trust had received almost £4 million from Union Carbide's former Indian unit but still needed a further £9.5 million to build and run its hospital for the victims. In 1988, after some four years of legal wrangling, the Indian state courts ordered Union Carbide to pay $515 million to the Indian Government to compensate the victims. The Supreme Court set the final compensation at $470 million. Later a lower court in Bhopal had Union Carbide's assets seized.

The scale of the disaster and the extent of human suffering has meant that Bhopal will remain in our minds for a long time. For boards it was a chilling example of what can happen not just in developing countries but also in the developed world. There was a sting in the tail. The Union Carbide executives were being pursued by politicians and the victims' families not just for compensation but for justice. Specifically, they wanted them indicted on corporate manslaughter charges which would have very serious consequences if they were found guilty. These charges have not been brought so far.

It is the big fear of many boards that they will wittingly, or unwittingly, so pollute the physical environment that they will not only have to pay compensation corporately but will also be held *personally* liable and so put their own assets at risk as well as risking imprisonment. Everybody realizes that there is a swelling tide of public opinion about protecting the physical environment against the encroachment on it by business, which is reinforced by the growing raft of legislation being enacted around the world. This is not yet another 'soft' issue on which liberally-minded boards can show largesse and reap the public relations benefits by being seen to be 'green'. It is a hard-edged issue. Polluting the waterways in Britain, developing non-recyclable packaging in Germany, greedily cutting hardwoods in Canada or Borneo, importing ivory from East Africa or Asia, can all lead boards to be held legally accountable. There is no 'limited liability' here.

In the UK regulatory authorities are increasingly prepared to prosecute individual company directors and employees for breaking environmental and health and safety laws. This growing trend seems to have been imported from the US where personal liability challenges are being used increasingly to highlight the dangers of a company's environmental performance. The consequences for directors are very serious. For indictable offences in the UK they can now be disqualified under the Directors Disqualification Act 1986 and the level of fines is rising rapidly. Directors cannot insure against such fines, although they may be able to obtain cover for legal costs. The personal stigma, and public relations consequences, of a conviction must be weighed very seriously. Convictions are not career enhancing.

The wording of certain UK Acts is the same as for criminal convictions. The Environmental Protection Act 1990, the Water Resources Act 1991, and the Health and Safety at Work Act 1974 are designed to catch directors, managers, company secretaries and other company officers where offences have been committed with their consent, connivance, or as a result of negligence. 'Manager' has been interpreted by the judges to extend only to those who have control over company policy or strategy. 'Consent' requires knowledge and agreement. 'Connivance' involves knowledge but doing nothing about it. 'Neglect' is wider and extends to failure to do things which a director knows, or ought to know, that he or she should do. One of the current concerns of UK directors and managers is that they will also be held *personally* responsible for clean-up costs. This is possible under civil law principles, and statute, but cases have been rare – so far.

Accountability for the physical environment is an international issue. It is not just a matter of trying to placate, or fend off, external 'green' pressure groups. A good example of how the future might develop in this area was seen in August 1993 when 273 fund managers in the City of London received a letter urging them not to invest in the Indonesian logging and wood production company Barito Pacific. Barito was allegedly planning a £179 million flotation on the Jakarta Stock Exchange. However this allegation was strongly denied by Barito. The letter led to some puzzlement among the fund managers who generally did not know what to do, especially as Salomon Brothers had withdrawn in July as lead underwriters. This was believed to be due to its concern about a lack of management information which it is obliged to supply to the US regulatory authorities.

Environmentalists and human rights pressure groups wanted to stop the growth of Barito, one of the world's leading suppliers of plywood, pulp and paper. Funds from the flotation were needed to boost the company's pulp production and its area planted to industrial forest. The environmentalists argued that the flotation was not in the interests of the environment, that large numbers of indigenous people had their lands logged by the company without consent, and that for the longer term there was no process of sustainable development of the Indonesian economy. The pressure groups, thirteen in total, included Greenpeace, Friends of the Earth and the Japanese Tropical Forest Action Network.

Fund managers are increasingly concerned if there are environmental clouds hanging over a share issue. Michael Hanson-Lawson, Managing Director of Crosby Securities UK, the flotation's international coordinator, said that the project was economically sound and he would not be swayed by the campaigners' arguments. He was, however, impressed by the efficiency of the campaign. He thought, though, that the campaign would be nothing more than a 'minor irritant'. The campaigners stressed that they would continue to target fund managers, and would attempt to use the City of London as a lever for bringing about change. They admitted that they had much to learn about influencing the City, and that although they were relative novices in the use of 'City' language, they intended to improve. Who said policy and accountability were soft areas for directors?

It is not just the developing world that causes environmental problems. Corporations are now suing corporations. The Prudential, Britain's largest life assurer, is suing PowerGen over its burning an environmentally controversial fuel in its Richborough, Kent power station. Prudential claims that the orimulsion fuel is damaging crops on one of its farms near the power station. The allegations have been strongly refuted by National Power. However, as this row blew up at the time when the PowerGen Chief Executive, Ed Wallis, was about to give evidence to the UK's House of Commons Select Committee on Employment who are investigating executive pay rises, it created particularly bad publicity for PowerGen. Orimulsion is a bitumen-based fuel from Venezuela which is imported cheaply as an alternative to coal. It is attacked by environmentalists as dirty, and has been accused of causing childhood asthma through its emission of nitrous oxide gas. It is also said to raise the levels of particles of nickel and vanadium in the atmosphere. Prudential is seeking 'substantial damages' for the 'peculiar form of damage' to its crops, alleging that vegetables have suffered lesions to their leaves and a reduced resistance to disease since PowerGen began burning orimulsion in 1990. Should the case be won by Prudential it would undermine National Power's plan to switch over its power stations to orimulsion, and so cripple the fuel's long-term future.

One of the most enlightening cases for boards to study has been the eruption of public emotion over the proposed sinking of the Shell and Conoco redundant Brent Spar oil platform in the North Atlantic in 1995. The Shell UK board realized that this was a delicate environmental and cost issue that went much wider than the rights and wrongs of sinking a single platform. There are around two hundred platforms and rigs to be disposed of in the North Sea alone. Shell had conducted exhaustive research on the qualities of toxins and non-toxic waste remaining in the rig. The best scientific evidence was that there would be less environmental damage sinking it in an Atlantic trench than trying to dispose of it on land. Shell UK duly sent out, as it was required to do as best practice, notice of its intentions and the supporting evidence to the governments around the North Sea and the East Atlantic seaboard. They had no responses. They felt reasonably safe that they could proceed on what would be a high profile disposal, and one about which the public would be very sensitive. The situation then began to gallop away from them rapidly, as shown opposite.

The Brent Spar affair is a classic case of a board having to balance policies and values against accountabilities. The use of logic, rationality and scientific evidence to reinforce these is understandable, particularly of people with an engineering/scientific or financial background where convergent thinking is the board norm. It thought that what it did was 'right' but it did not use any noticeable 'divergent' thinking to 'reframe' the problem and the contexts, especially the range of people who could claim to be, or claim to represent, 'stakeholders'. As *The Financial Times* of 5 July 1995 put it: 'In the course of a few weeks Shell stumbled so badly over

Table 8   Sequence of events in the Brent Spar affair

1976   Brent Spar becomes operational

1991   Brent Spar stops operations

1995   *17 February*
UK energy minister Tim Eggar approves the plan to sink the platform in the Atlantic

30 April
Greenpeace activists gain access to the platform in the North Sea

15 May
Activists defy court order to move

22 May
Shell, with police support, attempts to board the platform but is stopped by rough seas

24 May
Greenpeace gives up its occupation peacefully

10 June
Shell tries to take the platform under tow – Shell employees and activists clash

15 June
German Chancellor Helmut Kohl criticizes Shell and threatens to bring the matter before the forthcoming G7 Conference

16 June
UK Prime Minister John Major defends Shell to Helmut Kohl at G7. Firebomb at Shell Germany petrol station in Hamburg. Two protestors board platform in Atlantic from a helicopter

19 June
UK Energy minister Tim Eggar calls the protestors highly irresponsible

20 June
Two more protestors land on platform by helicopter. Shell abandons plans to sink the platform

28 August
Channel 4 News admits it was 'bounced' by Greenpeace's videotapes

5 September
Greenpeace admits its analysis of the pollutants on the platform was wrong and apologizes publicly to Shell

an environmental issue that it alienated nearly all of its corporate constituencies.'

Did the board ever see them clearly as constituencies? The environmental activists knew that their members bouncing around the ocean in Zodiac dinghies with a huge oil platform in the background would make 'good television' and, therefore, get headlines. Activists landing on the platform and being fought off was even better TV. The landing of activists by helicopter on the floating rig was a public relations coup which ensured that the issue stayed in the headlines in Europe and the US. The UK government was determined to stand by Shell UK's decision despite some national criticism that it was not being strong enough with Shell over its declared policy of 'the polluter pays' for all environmental issues. However, they appear to have underestimated two external environmental issues, both of which should have been picked up by their monitoring systems.

The first was that Shell itself is increasingly becoming organizationally a 'federal' structure. What Shell UK does is its own business, but only to an extent. Shell Germany was beginning to get worrying information on the effect of the sales ban called by environmentalist groups. Second, Chancellor Kohl was not politically strong at home and with only a two-seat majority on his coalition government was in desperate need of additional support, particularly from the 'Green' party. So although, like the other governments, he had said nothing about Shell UK's proposal at the time, he now played them as a political card for his party interests. On 15 June 1995 he had obliquely warned Shell UK of the dangers of continuing with the disposal: 'If I were a company I would not do anything which hurt my business'. After that the firebombing of a Shell petrol station in Hamburg seemed to firm his, and the public's, opinion that Shell Germany was now seemingly opposed to its Chancellor. A main board meeting of the Royal Dutch Shell Group was called in The Hague where they agreed to instruct Shell UK to abandon the disposal plan. This brought them relief from the generally bad publicity, and from pressure from the German Chancellor. Chris Fay, head of Shell UK, explains their thinking at the main board meeting: 'Shell UK's position was not tenable, but that of the group as a whole was.' He believed that people in the UK did not appreciate the emotional and violent reactions which the Brent Spar affair had caused in Germany. He then had to face an infuriated UK government who had supported him, and who were now much less likely to be sympathetic to Shell and much more likely to ensure that 'the polluter pays'.

Greenpeace won the major battle of the public relations war. Whether this was wise is yet to be proved. New independent figures suggest that the sinking, whilst polluting the Atlantic for a short period, might even have helped some of the deep water creatures which live in the trench as they live on some of the 'pollutants'. With Shell now having to find ways of disposing of the rig on land, there are a great number of very dangerous jobs to be created and the physical environmental pollution costs of such work are likely to be much higher than the sinking. Fay says that for business the big issue which has come out of the Brent Spar incident is the degree to which a highly-focused *single-issue* campaign can undermine the most carefully laid out and scientifically sound plans.

I would add two points. First, that boards have to deal increasingly with a number of political pressures and *emotional* climates when coping with the board issue of stakeholder accountability. Second, that it is still quite easy to fool the media with dramatic, hand-held video pictures. In the *Financial Times* of 28 August 1995 the Head of Channel 4 News in the UK admitted that they 'were bounced' by Greenpeace by being given such videos and showing them quickly. They would have done better, he said, to have reviewed the scientific evidence first and carried that simultaneously. This is something for all boards to ponder.

On 5 September Greenpeace admitted publicly that it had made errors in estimating the amount of oil left in the rig. Lord Melchett, Chairman of Greenpeace, wrote to Shell saying, 'We have realized in the past few days that when the samples were taken the sampling device was still in the pipe leading to the storage tanks, rather than in the tanks themselves. I apologize to you and your colleagues for this.' Dr Fay of Shell UK is reported to have said, 'We respect Greenpeace for admitting the mistake. It is a step in the right direction.' However, all was not so calm on the UK Government's side. Tim Eggar, the Energy minister, accused Greenpeace of being untrustworthy and prone to fabricating information for its own ends. He said, 'I always said [Greenpeace's] wild allegations were not based on fact. This proves it. Greenpeace claims it acted responsibly by admitting its mistake. It only did so because it knew it would be found out.' Greenpeace's credibility has been dented which, for a voluntary organization, could be serious as it relies on public subscriptions. Let us hope that all sides learn from this unedifying use of the media to put across a complex case about environmental pollution and conservation as a simple, emotional, televisual issue. For Shell UK it has thrown its accountability to stakeholders into question.

ENSURING BOARD AUDITS

Under most legislations boards are held accountable through, at the very minimum, the publication of an annual set of reports and accounts. These are meant to give the owners an overview of the business's performance over the past year, as well as a taste of the future. All those countries who want to participate in world trade in the twenty-first century aspire to some form of transparency, but it varies dramatically around the world. China, which will be a massive player in the twenty-first century, still has not agreed or installed its internationally accepted accounting systems and standards, nor does it yet have a robust system of commercial laws and a process for their enforcement.

A Learning Board will need to do much more than the minimum. Most boards will follow the Cadbury, or Viénot, or OECD ideas.

They will appoint a series of Committees of the Board. I hate the word 'committee' as it implies a procedurally-driven, long-lived, bureaucratic group dedicated to administrative process rather than thoughtful direction-giving. Why not call them 'work groups' and give them a 'use-by' date?

The Cadbury-style committee system is the best-tested. It comprises:

An Audit Committee to oversee the finances
A Nominations Committee to agree on selection for the board
A Remuneration Committee to agree the pay and benefits package for the board

I notice that, in addition, many boards aspiring to become Learning Boards are appointing other audit working groups for such issues as:

Environmental audit
Crisis management/contingency planning audit
Intellectual property generation and registration audit
People development audit
Health and safety at work audit

Some enterprises, like ICI and British Gas, already publish separate annual accounts of their environmental performance.

The lawyers Cameron Markby Hewitt give examples (shown overleaf in Table 9) of the sorts of areas about which the environmental or health and safety at work audit work groups should be concerned.

I have now completed my review of the cycle of the tasks of the board's year:

Formulating Policy
Strategic Thinking
Supervising Management
Accountability

Table 9   Main areas for Environmental Health and Safety at work audit

Insurance	Such cover as is available should be in place
Education	Programmes should be arranged to ensure that everybody knows their duties
Management Systems	An environmental and/or crisis management system is advisable. BS 7750 or the EC Eco-Audit Scheme are useful starting points but may need adapting. Our experience has been that these systems can often operate as useful mitigation in prosecutions and may afford a complete answer if a due diligence defence is available
Financial Management	Environmental liabilities need to be properly quantified and provided for in a company's accounts so that future problems do not affect viability. Some methodical approach is advisable
Due Diligence	On acquisition directors should bear in mind that if they take environmental risks on purchasing new businesses they may become personally liable. Thorough due diligence is essential.

Source: Cameron, Markby, Hewitt 1995

I hope that you will be in no doubt by now that direction-giving is not an optional 'add on' to the senior management role. Being a member of a Learning Board is a job in itself which needs careful preparation, training, development, and assessment. Not everybody can do it. Not everybody wants to do it, although many would like the pay and benefits package usually associated with it.

How do we go about developing ourselves for this crucial job?

CHAPTER 7

Development Processes for Boards and Directors

There are three pre-conditions if the board development process is to be successful. First, the board members must recognize the difference between 'managing' and 'directing'. Second, they must appreciate the need from the start to 'benchmark' the position of the board as a working group, themselves as individual board members, and the organization itself, both in terms of where they are now, and where they wish to be. These 'differential' measures are the foundation of any type of development process. Third, the chairman must take responsibility for the board development processes.

Once these conditions are established, my experience shows that there are seven fundamental needs which must be addressed before the board can become effective.

Seven Development Needs for Directors

For the individual director these are:

1. An independence of thought and action when undertaking the direction-giving role.
2. Competence when handling the four Dilemmas - in other words, the capacity to be responsible and yet detached; to deal with both the concrete and the abstract.
3. Being able to take the 'helicopter view' – viewing board issues from various perspectives.

4. A portfolio of thinking styles to cope with the diversity of board issues – a capacity to rise above convergent, or binary, thinking processes.
5. Being comfortable with reflecting upon and debating issues and developing scenarios without having to take immediate action.
6. Making the connection between policy and strategic thinking decisions, being able to implement them, and being able to learn from the results.
7. The ability to time-budget for the process of direction-giving as distinct from managing.

For the board as a whole there is a particular need to learn how to work as an effective, reflecting, debating and decision-making group.

How does one develop such paragons of excellence? To those outside the board it seems that once a director has been given the job title they should move miraculously from being a crisis-driven senior manager, or professional, to suddenly becoming omniscient. Whereas before they were so head down that they missed most things, now they know everything and can do everything including leaping mountains at one bound.

It does not feel like that inside the board. A surprising number of directors with whom I have worked have said how lonely the post is. This is particularly true of chief executives. They report frequently that they do not have reliable sources of information to let them know what is happening inside the enterprise because everyone has a vested interest in slanting information for maximum personal advantage. One of the most senior CEOs with whom I have ever spoken described himself as sitting in a magnificent office with a set of levers of power in front of him. People were in awe of the power he had through these levers and assumed quite subservient behaviours towards him. But, as he said, 'I can pull these levers of power but I really do not know if they are connected. The organizational response time is longer than my patience, so I will tend to intervene again before things move into action. This often kills initiative or learning. It is frustrating all round.'

Boards are rarely teams, even though they often refer to themselves as 'top teams'. They seldom spend a significant amount of time together and so do not develop the attitudes and skills of those who do work continuously alongside each other. Boards are typically groups of powerful individuals who come together for legalistic and administrative reasons – the board meeting – then fly apart. Getting them to see the need to be an effective working group when they are together is an essential part of the board, and individual director, development process.

Building Blocks for the Board

Dick Giordano, once CEO of British Oxygen Company and now the reforming Chairman of British Gas, has outlined five building blocks for board development:

1. COMMITMENT TO THE UNITARY BOARD

The UK practice, where all directors are equal, gives the best chance of creating an effective board. US boards, which are closer to the German two-tier board model, have the problem that their major strategic decisions and tactics are *management* decisions, not the board's, and can easily become too tactical and short-term, particularly if they are too deeply interwoven with the internal politics of the enterprise.

Within the unitary board there is a need for total clarity about the differing roles of the chairman and chief executive. Giordano's definition is that the chairman is the 'boss of the board' whilst the CEO is the 'boss of the company's operations'. This ensures that there is a continual balancing of powers between the chairman and the CEO and between the executives and the independent directors. Directors should be reminded regularly that 'a director is a director. Just that'.

2. A GOOD DIRECTOR SELECTION PROCESS

The selection of directors, especially independent directors, must be made on the basis of good board experience of industry and experience in life. They must have the self-confidence to stand up to others. It is not necessary to balance the numbers of executive directors and independent directors evenly. Grand Metropolitan plc, for example, has powerful executive directors who run international brands such as J & B Whisky, Burger King, Pilsbury, Häagen-Dazs ice cream, Jose Cuervo tequila, Baileys Irish Cream, Aqua Libra, and Hueblein beer, and only three independent directors: David Simon, Head of BP, Sir Colin Marshall, Head of British Airways, and Dick Giordano, Head of British Gas. These three give the executive directors a good, critical, run for their money at any time.

3. COMMITMENT TO ORGANIZING THE COMPANY'S AFFAIRS FROM THE BOARDROOM

Directors must make adequate preparation beforehand on all board agenda items, and the chairman must create sufficient time for questions, debate and consensus checking. This can cause frustration. Executive directors do not always appreciate the need to slow down to 'pick up' the independent directors and debate with them, and then slow down again to drop them off for another month. It is the chairman's job to ensure that the executive directors are trained to appreciate and value this process as it is essential to a well-performing board.

4. A CHAIRMAN IN PLACE WHO KNOWS HIS OR HER JOB.

Despite the Cadbury and Greenbury Committees' reports, this is not always the case – some cannot differentiate between the content of board discussion and the process by which the chairman controls that discussion. The *chairing* process of the board meetings, and the preparatory work with the CEO and company secretary to ensure that brief, literate board papers are sent out well ahead of time, means that the chairman must have the time and inclination to do this well, and must be paid appropriately for it.

The chairman must also have the stature, personal attitudes, skills and self-confidence to influence the powerful players on the board. There will always be powerful players, which is why it can never be a true 'team together'. It is to the diversity of these powers that the wise chairman will play, thus ensuring sufficient variety in the board's thinking before decision-taking.

5. PROPER STRATEGIES DEVELOPED BY THE BOARD UNDER THE CHAIRMAN

At the very minimum there must be clearly articulated business and financial strategies. For this to work well the chairman must take responsibility to ensure that:

- Executive directors do not have fixed, single solutions, vetted elsewhere, that they simply bring to the board for approval. There is a need for questioning, debate and understanding by the board, which means taking time off-site to get to grips with the strategic thinking issues.
- An appropriate performance measurement system is in place, and is always allocated sufficient time on the board agenda.
- The key discipline of ensuring adequate directoral and managerial succession and development is agreed and in place.

- Special issues or projects are on the board agenda and are vetted regularly to ensure that they can be accurately transmitted to the board's various constituencies.
- Effective use is made of the board's time within, and between, meetings. This is best achieved by:
  - Keeping the agenda short.
  - Keeping a clearly understood system of performance indicators.
  - Keeping a system by which the independent directors can check information and facts between and before a board meeting.
  - Ensuring that the agenda is stuck to once it is agreed with the CEO and company secretary.
- The independent directors are kept informed of, and understand, their role – not as policemen in a two-tier structure, but as members of a unitary board in which the business will invest for their own development.
- The executive directors benefit from investment in their development.

METHODS OF TRAINING AND DEVELOPMENT

It is worth reiterating two things before we start.

First, the ultimate responsibility for ensuring that directors are trained to competence, then developed continuously, is that of the chairman. This is one of the three paramount activities for the chairman – the other two being to chair the board effectively, and knowing when to sack the chief executive.

Second, that there is a major distinction between 'training' and 'development'.

Training is a necessary and often relatively mechanical process by which a blend of knowledge, attitudes and skills is identified to ensure competence in a carefully defined job. Appropriate learning processes are devised which allow the person involved to reach, and be assessed as having reached, the necessary competences. In most businesses the training of directors is not taken very seriously partly because it has not been easy to specify the job precisely. The publication of the IOD *Standards* has changed that. The subsequent IOD *Standards Workbook* defines the basis of director training. A logical extension of this definition is that, over time, assessment of trained directors will become normal, a register of competent directors will be established, and directors' educational and practical competencies will be linked to their appearance on such registers, at least for listed companies. Directing will begin to have some of the characteristics of a recognized profession – including systematic training and continuous professional development.

Development differs from training in that it focuses on the individual rather than the job. 'Development' comes from the Latin root *volupe* and is about two related aspects. First, identifying the 'richness' contained within a person or thing. Second, making this potential manifest and putting it to good use.

The paucity of trained directors around the world means that board efforts must first be focused on training. Only when this is established can the board be brought up to competence in other areas.

A board needs to commit itself to the idea of having three parallel streams of training and development under way simultaneously:

The training and development of individual directors
The training and development of the board as an effective working group
The continuing development of the enterprise as a whole

The output of each of these three developmental processes must be seen to feed into the other two both to ensure value is being added by the investments in time and money, and that each process becomes self-managing and self-correcting. These three developmental processes are central to the long-term *learning*, and therefore essential to the survival and growth, of the enterprise. They are the heart of the Learning Board and, consequently, the Learning Organization.

Benchmarking and Assessment

Benchmarking should happen at the start of any developmental process, but the benchmarking, or assessment, of directors is a difficult issue. Directors' fears that any form of assessment will find them lacking in some areas is likely to be true. Given the percentage of those not trained to direct, this is hardly surprising. But notice that I choose deliberately to use the word 'assessment' rather than 'selection'. I work with what I am given, and encourage organizations to do the same. The question at present is what to do with the directors we have.

The methods of assessment and selection range from interviewing, psychometric testing and the use of assessment/development centres to the decidedly weird and woolly like graphology (highly favoured in France) and astrology (frequently found in Asia and a few parts of the US). Dr Mike Smith of UMIST shows in Fig. 20 (opposite) the validity coefficients between the assessment processes available.

My own preference is to start with benchmarking the board as a whole, taking individual scores through psychometric tests but concentrating on the pattern for the total board rather than the individuals. Doing this in the open in front of the whole board can be a most liberating process for all board members, including the chairman and chief executive, because once it is legitimate to talk about, map and value differences it is surprising how intra-board politics calms down. When individual benchmarking starts, the directors can respect each other's differences, understand that others think and behave in ways different from themselves, and play to

A GUIDE TO
(CORRECTED) VALIDITY COEFFICIENTS

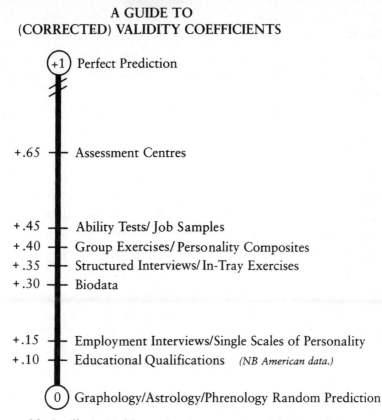

Figure 20 Saville & Holdsworth's Assessment Validity Coefficients

Source: Dr Mike Smith, UMIST

their own and others' strengths rather than trying to 'clone'. Diversity amongst directors can be acknowledged as a good thing, reinforcing the Learning Board.

This early benchmarking usually takes one or two 'awaydays' – the whole board must agree on its needs for development in the four main areas: Policy Formulation, Strategic Thinking, Supervision of Management and Accountability.

Attention can then turn to two central aspects of a board's capabilities:

Their range of thinking styles.

Their ability to work together as an effective group.

There are many validated psychometric inventories for doing this, although cultural bias always needs to be checked on them. One new piece of software has nearly two hundred psychometrics on it, and can be driven by a non-psychologist if they follow the instructions explicitly. I prefer to have a psychologist overseeing both the process and the interpretation of the data.

Using the software one can select up to nine competencies at one time in groups appropriate to the various directoral roles of the board. The individual director scores these onto their personal computer and feeds them back to a central compiler in total confidence. The aggregated responses are then brought to the board for discussion, benchmarking, and agreement on ways to advance the three integrated development processes.

I prefer to work with the board in real time, debating these issues as a work group. The specific developmental needs of the individual directors, however, are best dealt with off-line, one-to-one, unless the director wants specifically to declare his or her development needs in front of the other directors. I am surprised how many do, asking the others to support them in bringing themselves up to competence.

In the early phases of integrated director development the pattern of response of the whole board remains my focus. Given the scores, what are the overdone strengths (which others will see as weaknesses)? Where are the significant gaps in their portfolio of thinking styles? Where are they cloned? Given what they are trying to achieve in the future, what personal resources do they have for thinking strategically, abstractly, and using the uncertainty to advantage? What personal resources do they have to translate strategic thinking into effective implementation?

Such discussions oil the working processes of the group and resolve the directors' guilt (particularly strong in the West) about not being omniscient. Each director needs to see where they add value to the board and how they would be 'shamed' for not doing so – a more Eastern approach and alien to many Westerners.

As I have said earlier, directing is essentially an intellectual activity. It is difficult to benchmark a board on its thinking capacities. The few tools there are tend to reflect analytical and problem-solving capacities rather than the manipulation of ideas and patterns. The only psychometric test I know of that deals with the range of thinking in a systematic way is the Thinking Intentions Profile.[39] In its most sophisticated form it looks at twenty-five types of thought and one's preferences in relation to these.

In its simplest form, it looks at six basic types of thinking:

Past-orientated thinking (judging what is right)
   logic/rationality
   values/commitment
Present-orientated thinking (describing what is true)
   the hard facts
   sensing the soft facts
Future-orientated thinking (realizing what is new)
   using ingenuity
   visionary capacity

As a crude generalization of directors globally, I would say that their tendencies are to be very strongly biased to the past-orientated thinking styles of logic and values/commitment; to make strong use of their sensing capacities to identify the soft facts of what is happening 'now', but underuse the hard facts; to have a strong sense of vision, but underuse ingenuity – their least preferred thinking style.

The tendency to underuse the hard facts and avoid ingenuity/implementation goes some way to explaining the persistent reports around the world of directors being out of touch with reality and prone to launching strategies which are not implementable.

Development Agendas

With this constructive and emotionally neutral approach to bench-marking boards and directors it is possible to create individual director, board, and enterprise *Development Agendas* which plan the training and development processes required for each party to reach the board's agreed needs. The chairman must monitor these regularly as mentor and/or coach to each director and to the board as a whole. If things go well, and using this approach they usually do, then board members can in time become more openly personal in the requests they make of each other to contribute more effectively to the board. Again, there are many simple approaches.

The next step is to use a 'Stop, Start, Continue' analysis. This can be as simple as hanging flipchart paper on the boardroom wall with the name of each director placed above the words 'Stop, Start, Continue'. The directors are encouraged to write in each of the three categories actions which would help that director be more effective on the board: what they should stop doing, what they should start doing, and what they should continue to do. This can be done anonymously at first, perhaps in a separate room during a mealtime or coffee break, but later it can become a legitimate part of a board meeting. Although there are more sophisticated methods, I have found this a robust way of getting to grips with effective group-working on boards around the world.

It is for the chairman to ensure that each director is properly mentored or coached, by themselves, by someone else within the organization, or through suitable outside help – an experienced and disinterested outsider. The Cadbury Committee recommended that this should include external legal advice for independent directors. Some companies are using recently retired independent directors. The mentor/coach can help identify alternative approaches to self-development, board role development, and routes along a career path.

Chairmen should ensure that a small time and money budget is made available for the personal well-being of each director. I have seen this give a tremendous positive boost to the emotional climate of the board. Applied across the company it affects the whole organizational culture, and hence the drive of the enterprise. It can be especially helpful for directors who have led an achievement-driven life and feel that there is a lack of balance in a number of personal areas: between mind and body, work life and home life, work and recreation, work life and spirit. The vast majority of directors I meet around the world think that they are out of balance on all of these dimensions and are struggling to find the time to rebalance matters. Having a Personal Development Agenda at least legitimizes the aspiration. If all members of the board agree on budgeting time to achieve this, it will be more likely to happen.

I became involved in the case of a bright young director of an enormously successful high-tech electronics company. He had rocketed to the top and was seen by everyone as a very high flyer. He worked long hours, coming into the office at around 8 a.m. and leaving at around 7 p.m., taking work with him at the weekends. In conventional terms he was successful. The company acknowledged this and promoted him rapidly, increased his salary, and gave him a very smart car with a driver. This encouraged him to move out of the city and let the driver take the strain of his travel. He bought a comfortable house in the countryside about forty miles out. Then he found that the traffic into the city was so bad in the mornings that the only way to do things comfortably was to get into the office at around 7 a.m. and leave at 8 p.m. He was able to do this because he had no children and he and his wife worked near each other so they could travel together.

But the consequences were devastating on his direct reports. He was a hard and demanding boss. They had sought his implicit approval by getting into the office just before him and leaving after him. His extended hours made this very difficult: the long hours they had to work caused problems both in their physical and mental capacities and in their family life. He did not appreciate that this was happening until the sickness and turnover rates rose above those of other sections of the business.

When he did realize, he sought help himself. It was agreed that he would do two things. First, make it absolutely clear to his staff that they would not lose face, or promotion prospects, if they worked normal hours: that it was the quality of their output he valued more than the quantity. Second, restructure his time to give himself some personal space. One thing he had always wanted to do was to learn to scuba dive. So it was agreed that he would have individual lessons at a local pool. This meant that he left the office at 6 p.m. at least two nights a week. He found that he enjoyed having more of a social life, and soon matters returned to a more balanced existence all round.

Unless these balances are struck then the fish really does start to rot from the head. The head sets the example for the organization as a whole.

For any director too narrow a fixation on work alone can be disastrous as personal diversity implodes. Some companies offer and pay for 'complementary medicine' approaches such as the Alexander Technique, or McTimoney chiropractic, or dietary and exercise help to combat the abuse of the mind and body at work. Others offer personal sports coaching, or 'The Inner Game' approach to sport, as ways of trying to ensure that a total fixation on work is avoided. Companies such as Corporate Health Consultants[40] offer a service of both individual director development and integrated board development, using a mixture of indoor and outdoor learning processes, centred around the board learning the thoughtful acceptance of challenge and the parallel generation of trust within their group. Challenge and trust are key developmental aspects for the board's primary role of ensuring both enterprise and prudent control.

The Range of Development Processes

At present there are very few acknowledged centres of excellence for director development around the world. Unfortunately the rapidly growing demand lays the field open to charlatans – it is wise to check the approach and experience of any potential provider that isn't well known, and speak with clients who have been through the process.

The Institute of Directors in London is one of the few major quality suppliers. Its links with Leeds Metropolitan University has created a world first 'alternative to the MBA' for directors – the Masters in Company Direction. This is for more experienced senior managers, and potential and practising directors, and involves working on live projects in their board and enterprise whilst undergoing formal education and assessment.

The London IOD has regional centres around the UK to provide for its long-running Diploma and Accredited Diploma programmes and its many other director-orientated activities. The Australian Institute of Company Directors has a good range of director development programmes, as does the New Zealand Institute of Directors. In Sweden the new Swedish Academy of Directors is running both national programmes and a three-week International Director Programme for directors from the developing world. In Hong Kong Professor Bob Tricker at Hong Kong University is running director development programmes and my own company, Organization Development Ltd, is running the Hong Kong Institute of Directors Diploma programme for the public and private sector in Hong Kong, the People's Republic of China, and South East Asia.

This list is not comprehensive but does give a flavour of the ways in which director training and development is growing around the world. It is still an essentially Anglophone activity, but interest is growing in East Asia and Continental Europe. Business schools are not much help at this level as they often do not offer director development processes. They are equipped to deliver the intellectual basis of management and organization studies but have rarely made the investment in developing the intellectual and learning delivery basis for directors and boards. This problem is exacerbated by the fact that most business schools still stick to classroom-based timetables, which do not offer enough flexibility in the types of learning available to boards facing high business demands in real time.

But although the supply of director training is at present limited, there is more on offer than the standard classroom lecture. Most of the options are actually more 'user friendly', allowing much greater participation, an essential part of learning for directors.

The full range includes:

1. Coaching and mentoring by the chairman or others.
2. Job rotation – either swapping your permanent board job for a specified period, or using a temporary assignment approach to ensure that over time each director, executive or independent, has a much deeper insight into the activities of all the director functions.
3. Job shadowing – pairing with another director, independent or executive, for a limited period, usually six months, to study how their part of the organization operates.
4. Secondments or exchanges – gaining experience outside normal working life through functional and/or international swaps, within the company, between companies or with voluntary organizations, often by becoming an independent director.
5. Reading and study groups. Although it is often said that directors and managers do not read anything, this is untrue. What is true is that they rarely budget time to read and reflect. As a consultant to HarperCollins Business Books I have the figures to show that, given time, they enjoy both reading and discussing what they read. As suggested earlier, if giving a board a particular book to study and then comment upon looks too

threatening at the start, try a weekly 'serious' newspaper or journal which they are expected to read, note, and comment upon regularly until it becomes a board norm for informing Policy Formulation and Strategic Thinking.

6. Open courses (off-site) – attending programmes to develop knowledge, attitudes and skills in an environment of high diversity, hearing the experiences of others outside your organization.

7. Tailored courses (off-site) – company-specific courses with less chance for diversity but more chance for focus on particular company issues.

8. On-site courses – company-specific programmes with less diversity and more chance of interruption.

9. Outdoor courses – ranging from yomping across Alaska or the Borneo rainforest to integrated 'challenge and trust' courses.

10. Self-managed learning – where the individual, in cooperation with a learning institution and coach, agrees a modular programme of self-study either for professional or personal development, with the option of a certificated award.

11. Action Learning programmes – a growing trend where either unitary groups – for example all chairmen or all CEOs – or mixed groups tackle a key issue, or issues, in real time, meeting frequently to discuss their learning, and rigorously and constructively criticizing each other in the process.[41]

Developmental processes can ensure that a director develops the relevant attitudes and skills to cope with balancing the Board Conformance and Board Performance demands. It is usually the Board Performance aspects – Policy Formulation and Strategic Thinking – which are underdeveloped, so creating a personal portfolio of performance-related thinking styles is crucial. Phil Hanford's map of strategic thinking learning processes, (see Fig. 21 overleaf), gives a useful overview of this area.

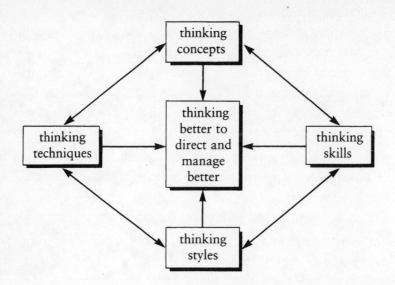

Figure 21 Phil Hanford's map of strategic thinking learning processes

At present the bulk of director development activities are training-based courses held off-site. Some four thousand directors have been through the IOD programmes since 1990, nearly a thousand of whom have completed the Diploma. The demand for follow-on continuing professional development has been such that an IOD Diploma Network has been set up by the participants. Some have demanded assessment and this has led to the recent institution of the IOD Accredited Diploma. It is early days yet but if the public demand for more professional directors continues to rise following the Cadbury, Greenbury and Hampel Committees' reports, then the IOD has positioned itself well.

A few adventurous companies have taken the IOD Diploma in-house. The first to do so was Securicor plc, the international security, telecommunications and distribution business. They have now put over a hundred of their directors from the main and subsidiary boards through the Diploma programme, tailored for their needs, over a two-year period. They ensured that each director chose when they wanted to attend each session and so increased the diversity of each group to give maximum input and learning opportunities whilst reducing the chances of groupthink. So far it is seen as highly successful. Peter Humphrey, the Group Personnel Director who sponsored the Diploma programme, reports that there has been a noticeable increase in the quality and depth of subsidiary and main board strategic thought and behaviour in the following areas:

Securicor Group brand emphasis

Clearer understanding of markets and business sectors

More strategic attention to the business development processes

More surefootedness in business planning

Management development now being included in the business planning process

Establishment of more effective organizational patterns

Full responsibility for Human Resources and trades union relationships being taken at company level

Integration of the IT systems within the businesses.

Expansion overseas now characterized by Communications technology and products as well as Security Services

Purchase of Hartsfield Manor as the corporate 'Centre of Excellence' rather than as a training centre

In the Autumn of 1995 the TSB Group plc, a financial services group, put all its top sixty directors through the IOD Diploma. Other interested companies are beginning to negotiate about what looks like a growing trend for boards.

This 'sheep-dip' approach is necessary as initial training to get all directors up to speed and speaking a common language whilst developing sufficient diversity of thought. This is healthy in the short term for today's circumstances, but questions must be asked to open up a wider range of delivery systems for existing and potential directors to suit their individual developmental needs.

Although present provision is small and fragmented, I am optimistic that two sources of growing demand for director development are pointing the way ahead. On the one hand the owner-directors of small and medium-sized organizations are increasingly seeing the need for a more professional approach to their businesses. On the other hand institutional investors and stock exchange-listing directors are also demanding professional directors. As there is a similar trend in government agencies, the issue of board and director development is likely to be a highly topical issue for the start of the twenty-first century.

CHAPTER 8

A New Future for Directors?

Things fall apart, the centre cannot hold.
LOUIS MACNEICE

Across the world the general public and politicians are realizing that matters cannot continue as they are for boards of directors. Public confidence in those charged with directing our institutions has eroded too significantly. The present 'club' system of director selection and remuneration is sufficiently degraded for the ever-increasing demands for accessible and transparent systems and processes to be taken seriously.

There are two significant pressures for change which will bring about a transformation.

First, the demand for more 'shareholder democracy' needs to be accommodated if boards are to answer the public's perception that boards tend to put their own interests before their shareholders'. This tendency is seen at its worst in large corporations in Japan where the managers and staff think and behave as if it belongs to them not the shareholders. Japanese shareholders face a continuing risk of having their interests diluted and marginalized. However, as politicians around the world press for wider share-ownership, employee shareholder schemes, tax-exempt share purchase schemes and other equity-widening schemes, there is an inevitable conflict because of the lack of shareholder voices, criticism and participation in most boards' directoral decision-making.

The weaknesses of using only the Annual General Meeting for agreeing policy and strategy, for voting directors on or off the board, and for agreeing directors' benefit packages are of growing public concern. Although small investors are encouraged by politicians to use their voice, they quickly become aware of their lack of say in such matters. So the spotlight is swinging towards the larger shareholders, particularly the institutional fundholders, who represent the smaller investors through the huge sums they manage on behalf of the many employee pension funds.

Until recently most institutional fundholders around the world have argued that their job is to maximize profits for their funds, not to concern themselves directly with the long-term thinking or short-term operations of a company. Such thinking is changing slowly. Recent interventions by Calpers in the US and RailPen in the UK are significant. Both encourage their fund managers to take an active interest in the company by *voting* on proposed policies, strategies and remuneration issues and make their votes known to shareholders. If the politicians really believe in the value of mass, small shareholdings as the basis of wealthier and more stable societies, then, paradoxically, it will be the institutional funds who will advance their cause using, if necessary, proxy votes at AGMs to propose alternative policies, strategies and benefits packages.

The second pressure for change is political intervention in corporate affairs on behalf of the general public, which is manifested increasingly through the growing debate on the 'shareholder/stakeholder' balance in corporate governance. Despite the reality of shareholder weakness, the public perception is of shareholder strength and insensitivity to the many other parties who feel that they have a 'claim' on the enterprise. These claims are not just party political rhetoric; politicians around the world have been adding laws and regulations to underpin these diverse 'stakeholders', who now include not only the shareholders but also the customers, staff, suppliers, physical environment and local communities. Although the powers of such stakeholders vary from country to country, the global trend is clear – stakeholders will have greater powers over corporate direction-giving as we enter the twenty-first century. Employment protection and compensation laws, product warranties, codes of ethical trading with suppliers, 'green' issues and more sensitivity to employment effects on local communities are all examples of the types of complex issues boards will have to grapple with in the future. Significantly, the superior performance of most 'green' and 'ethical' funds are influencing both fund managers and boards to move in this direction.

So the push by both shareholders and other stakeholders for clarity of, and a say in, policies and strategies will bring about greater transparency and more open and constructive criticism of the board's thinking processes and actions. This will cause great resentment on many boards as their performance is dissected and commented upon by a wider public. Increasing international pressure for board transparency, whilst maintaining business confidentiality, will make such resistance ultimately useless. However, as I have shown before, many boards are not geared to learning quickly, and the simple fact that many boards do not understand the roles and tasks of direction-giving will be exposed. This will generate public, and political, demand for boards and directors to become 'more professional'.

Professionalization comes in many shades but there are two key aspects that need consideration. First, the need for an agreed and publicly accountable director assessment and registration process. Second, an agreed and policeable code of conduct to determine the ethical relationships between directors, shareholders and stakeholders. Many directors will be horrified by the thought of either, let alone both. They will argue that as you can become a 'director' simply by forming a legal corporate entity, or buying it off the shelf, then it is impossible to turn directing into a profession. They are right, and wrong. They are correct in that unless we change the whole basis of our laws on the possession of corporate ownership rights there will always be those who can buy a directorship and then decide if they will be bothered about becoming competent in direction-giving. That is their choice, and they must live with the consequences.

But they are wrong in that there are two strong forces pushing for the professionalization of directors. One is the self-esteem of many directors themselves. As I travel the world I am impressed by the growing numbers of directors, many but not all of them young, who recognize the difference between being a competent manager or professional and being a competent director on a truly Learning Board. The rapid growth of *voluntary* director training and development programmes, especially in Commonwealth countries, is a highly encouraging sign of the way ahead.

The second force will be seen in those companies listed on stock exchanges. Disillusion amongst shareholders, fund managers and politicians has influenced the listings directors of many stock exchanges. I expect to see, over the next decade, the start of a director accreditation and registration process for directors of listed companies in such places as London, Frankfurt, New York, Hong Kong and Sydney. This will not mean a 'big bang' introduction of mandatory accreditation and registration on all existing directors. It will most likely emerge as an insistence that all *new* directors are assessed as suitable for registration, possibly international registration. This is bound to create a lot of heated debate. I see the process as inevitable because of the historic lack of self-regulation of directors, even of listed companies. Directors have left themselves wide open to externally-imposed regulation and will now have to pay the painful price.

The issue of accreditation and registration is just becoming visible:

- Codes of conduct exist in Australia and are being debated in the United Kingdom, where the Cadbury, Greenbury and Hampel Committees are putting more codification into place, albeit on a voluntary basis.
- Registers of accredited directors are being discussed by stock exchanges and directors' institutes.

- An agreed body of knowledge, attitudes and skills is being developed in a number of countries. The UK's *Standards for the Board* is the vanguard here.
- Accreditation processes are being developed for the assessment of directors', and boards', knowledge, attitudes and skills. The IOD London and Leeds Business School's processes are giving the lead here.

I feel sure that the basic director accreditation and registration structure will not be mandatory in the first instance. It will start voluntarily and remain so for at least a decade as it is refined. If it later becomes mandatory, say in listed companies and public enterprises, it must start with new directors only, and with plenty of warning so that the new multi-media technologies can bring distance learning into play to cope with the inevitably vast increase in demand for director training and development.

That accreditation will come is inevitable. The question is when, and in which countries. My prediction of ten years is a very rough average. The public's growing intolerance of directoral ignorance and incompetence argues for a rapid implementation of professionalization. The public's growing repulsion of seemingly endemic directoral corruption in major companies in, for example, France and Italy, also pushes for rapid and radical reform. Even in the more staid Germany, 'relationship-based' corporate governance problems linked to cases of lack of directoral competence are beginning to erode public confidence in some of the companies which have been world leaders in excellence since 1945.

The 1995 OECD Report on Corporate Governance in Germany outlines some of the external factors that could make the convergence of the German and Anglo-Saxon models and other changes quite likely in the early twenty-first century:

- The internationalization of individual companies and the economy in general, which could prompt changes to information and accounting policies as foreign investors become more active, and as local companies become more active in securing finance abroad. In both cases international investors seek clarity and consistency of financial information.

- Increased internationalization of regulatory standards.
- The financing of new knowledge-based companies with heavy investments in intangible capital will require financing methods other than traditional bank finance relying on collateral.
- Institutional forms of saving could come to play a more significant role.

This list could apply not just to Germany but, for example, to Hong Kong, Japan, Malaysia, Mexico or the United Kingdom. Such external pressures for change will inevitably highlight the competence of boards of directors as a key benchmark for investing in a company. By demanding more clarity of information and consistency of reporting standards, I feel sure that we will see a universal model of corporate governance evolve with the UK's 'unitary board' emerging as the preferred option. It will be charged with both driving the enterprise forward and keeping it under prudent control within the demands made by shareholders and stakeholders.

I hope that in the balancing of shareholder and stakeholder demands the Anglo-Saxon mindset of business as a 'finite game' – win or lose, based on short-term, bottom-line driven results – will itself evolve towards the idea of business as an 'infinite game', of continuous learning from success and failure over the long term. Then we will see the widespread establishment of Learning Boards, able to cope with all the Directors' Dilemmas, and determined to prevent any fish rotting from the head.

Notes

1. Institute of Directors, *Development of and for the Board* (London, 1990).
2. John Argenti, *Corporate Collapse: Causes and Symptoms* (New York, McGraw-Hill, 1976).
3. Lawrence Peter, *The Peter Principle* (London, Pan Books, 1989).
4. Jan Carlzon, *Moments of Truth* (Ballinger, Cambridge, Mass, 1987).
5. Formal Investigation into the Herald of Free Enterprise, (HMSO, 1987).
6. Michael Frese, unpublished thesis (Germany, Giessen University, 1994).
7. The Hospitals Internal Communications Project, by Professor G.F. Weiland. This important report is one of the few social studies subject to long-term assessment and evaluation. Sadly it has been long out of print. However it is well reported in: *Hospitals: Communications, Choice, and Change*, ed. R.W. Revans (London, Tavistock Publications, 1971). The paper 'The Hospital as a Learning System' in *Action Learning: New Techniques for Management* by R.W. Revans (London, Blond and Briggs, 1980) is also well worth reading.
8. R.I. Tricker, *Corporate Governance* (London, Gower Press, 1980).
9. Gary Hamel and C.K. Prahalad, 'Strategic Intent', *Harvard Business Review*, May/June 1989.
10. Clifford Geertz, *The Interpretation of Cultures* (New York, Basic Books, 1973).
11. W.R. Ashby, 'Self-Regulation and Requisite Variety' in *Introduction to Cybernetics* (London, Wiley, 1956).
12. Charles Handy, *The Gods of Management* (London, Pan, 1985).
13. Fons Trompenaars, *Riding the Waves of Culture* (London, Nicholas Brearley, 1993).
14. Geert Hofstede, *Culture's Consequences* (California, Sage, 1980).
15. Geert Hofstede, *Cultures and Organizations: The Software of the Mind* (London, HarperCollins, 1994).
16. 'Making high ideals work on the ground', *Financial Times*, 6 April 1994.
17. Colin Sworder, 'Hearing the baby's cry' in *Developing Strategic Thought*, ed. Bob Garratt (London, McGraw-Hill, 1995).
18. Henry Mintzberg, *The Rise and Fall of Strategic Planning* (New York, Free Press, 1994).
19. Henry Mintzberg, 'Strategic thinking as "seeing"' in *Developing Strategic Thought*, op. cit.

20. Michael Porter, *Competitive Advantage* (New York, Free Press, 1980).

21. Ibid.

22. Sun Tzu, *The Art of War* (London, Penguin, 1992).

23. 'Plane Talking', *Financial Times*, 24 February 1995.

24. Charles Hampden-Turner, 'Strategic dilemmas occasioned by using alternative scenarios of the future' in *Developing Strategic Thought*, op. cit.

25. The Cadbury Committee, *The Financial Aspects Of Corporate Governance* (London, Gee & Co, 1992).

26. KPMG note to clients, May 1995, reported in 'Internal Controls Are The Real Issue', *The Times*, 20 July 1995.

27. Kao Corporation, 'Discovery Driven Planning', *Harvard Business Review*, July/August 1995.

28. The Cadbury Committee, op. cit.

29. 'More Room At The Top for Internal Audit', *Financial Times*, 9 February 1995.

30. Professor Richard Taffler, 'Putting future company disasters in the frame', *Financial Times*, 15 June 1995, referring to his paper, 'The Use of the Z-score Approach in Practice' (London, City University Business School, 1995).

31. The Conference Board, 'Corporate Boards: Improving and evaluating performance' (New York, 1994).

32. Adolph Berle and Gardiner Means, *The Modern Corporation and Private Property* (New York, Harcourt Brace, 1967).

33. 'Troubled Souls', *The Economist*, 6 January 1996.

34. John Galsworthy, *A Man of Property*, 1906.

35. Letter in *The Times*, 11 August 1994.

36. 'Unilever concedes detergent, damaged clothing', *Financial Times*, 23 September 1994.

37. Chris Argyris, *Knowledge in Action* (San Francisco, Jossey-Bass, 1993).

38. Charles Handy, *The Age of Uncertainty* (London, Business Books, 1989).

39. The Thinking Intentions Profile is sold under licence after training by Jerry Rhodes, Cotswold House, 16 Bradley Street, Wotton-under-Edge, Glos GL12 7AR, UK. Fax: 44 1453 521686.

40. Corporate Health Consultants can be contacted via Suzie Morel, The Old Rectory, St Brides-super-Ely, Near Cardiff, South Wales, UK. Fax: 44 1446 760050.

41. See Krystyna Weinstein, *Action Learning* (London, HarperCollins, 1995).

Useful Addresses

The Institute of Directors
Centre For Director Development
116 Pall Mall
London SW1
Tel. 44 0171 839 1233
Fax. 44 0171 930 1949

The Australian Institute of
Company Directors
71 York Street
Sydney NSW 2000
Australia
Tel. 612 9299 8788
Fax. 612 9299 1006

The Institute of Directors of New
Zealand
Level 3
South British Building
236 Lambton Quay
PO Box 7436 Wellington
New Zealand
Tel. 644 499 0076
Fax. 644 499 9488

The Institute of Directors of Hong
Kong
c/o Organisation Development
Ltd.
17/F Wyndham Place
40-44 Wyndham Street
Central
Hong Kong
Tel. 852 2868 3332
Fax. 852 2868 5366

The Swedish Academy of Directors
Svärdvägen 15
S-182 33 Danderyd
Sweden
Tel. 468 755 2527
Fax. 468 755 2586

Institutional Shareholder Services
Inc.
7200 Wisconsin Avenue
Suite 1001
Bethesda
Maryland MD 20814
USA
Tel. 301 718 2252
Fax. 301 718 2252

Acknowledgements

This book completes a trilogy. I would like to thank Helen Fraser of Fontana (now HarperCollins) for commissioning the first – *The Learning Organisation: and the need for directors who think* (1986); Phoebe Kynaston of Director Books for persuading me to create a special version for the Institute of Directors – *Creating A Learning Organisation: A guide to leadership, learning and development* (1990), which became *Learning to Lead* (1991) in the HarperCollins series; Lucinda McNeile, who commissioned *The Fish Rots from the Head* (1996) and who ensured that all three books are in print, and Juliet Van Oss for being such a constructive editor.

Given the global public concern about board and director ineffectiveness, it is surprising that there is only a small group of people who are director development specialists, and to them I would like to extend my professional and personal thanks for the support and enthusiasm they have provided during the writing of this book. In Hong Kong, Bob Tricker at Hong Kong University and my partner Peter Barrett at Organisation Development Ltd have been constructive critics; in Australia, Denise Fleming of Foresight Ltd, Phil Hanford of the MORE Centre, Shann Turnbull; Sir Bruce Watson, Fran Morris and Graham Stubington of the Australian Institute of Company Directors have all commented helpfully on my ideas and practices, as have Geoffrey Bowes of the Institute of Directors in New Zealand, Jamie Heard of Institutional Shareholder Services Inc. in the United States, Max Boisot and Jose-Maria D'Anzizu in Barcelona, Nils Ekblad and Tjorborn Ek at the Swedish Academy of Directors in Stockholm, and Henry Mintzberg in Canada. In the United Kingdom, my thanks go out to John Harper, Director of the Centre for Director Development at the Institute of Directors, and to Tim Melville-Ross and John Jackson there; to Sir Douglas Hague, Colin Coulson-Thomas, Thomas Clarke, Chris Peirce, Barry Curnow, John Lloyd and Charles Hampden-Turner; and to Sir Adrian Cadbury for his long-standing support. Many of these people have contributed essays to *Developing Strategic Thought* (London, McGraw-Hill, 1994), for which I am most grateful.

None of this would have been possible without the courage and imagination of the in-company folk who risked their reputations by letting me loose on their boards of directors, and who gave me robust feedback at all times. I would particularly like to thank Theresa Barnett and Sir Nicholas Goodison of TSB Group, Hugh Freedberg of Hill Samuel, Chris Davies of Sun Life Assurance, Dr Simon Chapman of The Medicine Group (Education), Lord Weinstock of The General Electric Company, David Kogan and Carolyn Wardrop-White of the National Health Service in Scotland, Pat Frost of the Fife Health Board, Lady Sally Irvine and Lionel Joyce of Newcastle City Health Trust, Mike Bett of British Telecommunications, Duncan Lewis of Mercury Communications, Roger Wiggs, Peter Humphrey and Peter Stansfield of Securicor, and Dr John Padfield, Howard Cork, and Tontschy Gerig of Glaxo Manufacturing. Around the world particular help was given in Hong Kong by C. H. Tung of OOCL, Hai Chi-yuet of Hongkong International Terminals, Stephen Ng and Yvonne Sun Siu of Wharf Cable, Paul Turton of Digital Systems Integration Asia Pacific, Chen De Rong of ICI China, Pengiran Ismail Mohamed of the ASEAN–EC Management Centre, Brunei, Darussalam, Paul McGrath of the Australian Maritime Safety Agency, John McGuigan of Baker and McKenzie, Chicago, and all the hundreds of participants in my *Organising for Tomorrow* seminars for the IOD in London and Hong Kong who tested the ideas and practices in the book and who proved my toughest critics.

Last but by no means least, a personal thank you to those who help keep me reasonably grounded in reality through the school of hard knocks that is corporate life: Rosalie Vicars-Harris and Malcolm Lewis of Media Projects International, who have asked me to chair the board of a creative and vibrant multimedia company riding the switchback of creating a business at the convergence of new technologies; and Peter and Mavis Barrett and Becky Law, my fellow board members at ODL Hong Kong. Sally Garratt, to whom I am married, gave quiet criticism, lots of support, and gave up her holiday so that I could find the days to write this book, needs very special acknowledgement, as does Margarete Hult, who lets me have Villa Gabrielle in Tourrettes-sur-Loup in the Côte D'Azur where there was peace and quiet enough to write it.

Thanks.

Bob Garratt
London
March 1996

Index